# Inside the Patent Factory

Laura McLeod .

# Inside the Patent Factory

## The essential reference for effective and efficient management of patent creation

### Donal O'Connell

John Wiley & Sons, Ltd

*Other Wiley Editorial Offices*

John Wiley & Sons Inc., 111 River Street, Hoboken, NJ 07030, USA

Jossey-Bass, 989 Market Street, San Francisco, CA 94103-1741, USA

Wiley-VCH Verlag GmbH, Boschstr. 12, D-69469 Weinheim, Germany

John Wiley & Sons Australia Ltd, 42 McDougall Street, Milton, Queensland 4064, Australia

John Wiley & Sons (Asia) Pte Ltd, 2 Clementi Loop #02-01, Jin Xing Distripark, Singapore
129809

John Wiley & Sons Canada Ltd, 6045 Freemont Blvd. Mississauga, Ontario, L5R 4J3 Canada

Wiley also publishes its books in a variety of electronic formats. Some content that appears in
print may not be available in electronic books.

*Library of Congress Cataloging-in-Publication Data*

O'Connell, Donal, 1963-
    Inside the patent factory : the essential reference for effective and efficient
management of patent creation / Donal O'Connell.
        p.  cm.
    Includes bibliographical references and index.
    ISBN 978-0-470-51640-9 (cloth : alk. paper)
    1. Patents.   2. Intellectual property – Management.   3. Industrial
property – Management.   I. Title.
    T212.O26 2008
    608 – dc22

                                                            2007050377


**British Library Cataloguing in Publication Data**

A catalogue record for this book is available from the British Library

ISBN 978-0-470-51640-9

Typeset in 11/16pt Trump Medieval by SNP Best-set Typesetter Ltd., Hong Kong
Printed and bound in Great Britain by TJ International Ltd, Padstow, Cornwall, UK

# Dedication

THIS BOOK IS DEDICATED TO EVERYONE WORKING IN Nokia's Intellectual Property Rights team, the inventor community across Nokia for your innovation and creativity, plus all of the Patent Agencies working on our behalf around the world

> *"Never doubt that a small group of thoughtful, committed people can change the world. Indeed, it is the only thing that ever has."* Unknown

# Contents

# Foreword

THIS IS A UNIQUE BOOK ABOUT INTELLECTUAL PROPERTY rights (IPR). The approach is new and the author, my good friend Donal O'Connell, is uniquely suited to analyse the creation of a patent portfolio based on his personal combination of experiences in product development, product creation and intellectual property. I hope that you enjoy the book and benefit from it.

My own experience in IPR stretches from the early 1980s to the present time. During this time the thinking in IPR has evolved from the casual protection of inventions, which happened to be made during development of practical products, to the current realisation that on the one hand IPR is a product in its own right and on the other hand it is possible, desirable, and in certain businesses even necessary to mass-produce such 'IPR products'. The times of the lonely, non-professional inventor belong to the past. Currently, innovations are cultivated and invention reports harvested in strategically defined target areas.

Nevertheless, the key to all IPR is the work of the creators, innovators and inventors. Their need and zeal to create new and improve existing products not only provides raw materials for the IPR factory, but also brings benefits to humans. The wish to climb the steps of the Hierarchy of Needs is still the driving force for most inventors. It is commonly stated that all great inventions arise from greed or laziness. I beg to differ slightly, as I believe in the inventor's internal search for satisfaction in providing better solutions, products and services. Money is of course important, but I have not seen any great differences between the productivity rates of inventors under different compensation systems. In my experience, non-monetary recognition is as important as monetary compensation. Both are needed.

Finally, let me emphasise the need to organise and manage the Patent Creation Factory in an efficient and streamlined way. All IPR, but especially patent creation, is very expensive and the teachings in this book should help by providing the live experiences in one company. The results may not be applicable to all, but at least these experiences are practical and tested in one application.

Urho Ilmonen
Chairman of the International Chamber
of Commerce, Intellectual
Property Commission

# Preface

THE BOOK IS TO ACT AS A COACHING MANUAL FOR anyone interested in intellectual property and those wanting to embark upon or develop their Patent Creation Factory. It draws on the author's own experience and insights from management and leadership, plus successful completion of a number of major change projects within a Patent Creation Factory unit.

The book guides the reader through each stage of setting up a successful unit and invites the reader to become actively involved by asking vital questions about their needs and aims.

Focusing on the key issues and themes involved for any Patent Creation Factory, it provides the reader with examples, diagrams and models to illustrate how theory can be put into practice. Topics include such issues as strategy development, the core activities of patent creation, key interfaces and relationships, possible organisational models and modes of operation, patent costs, patent quality, internal and external allocation of tasks and the techniques for properly managing external resources.

The book highlights how knowledge and innovation can be used and protected, which due to the increased importance of intellectual property rights, especially the use of patents, is essential in the business world. It also covers some of the changes taking place in the world of intellectual property, and how these may impact you.

The purpose is to encourage readers to challenge their own current Patent Creation Factory strategy, organisational structure and mode of operation by introducing various concepts, ideas, methods and tactics. It then offers advice and guidance on the pros and cons of the options presented and how any changes planned can be successfully implemented.

My hope is that this book really does get used – and used often – and does not just sit on the shelf after one read through.

**insidethepatentfactory@hotmail.co.uk**

# Acknowledgements

THE 'INSIDE THE PATENT FACTORY' PROJECT TOOK OVER two years from original idea right through to publication of the book. That period was taken up with research, phone calls, e-mails, face-to-face meetings, discussions, debate and revisions. One could argue, however, that the seed was planted for this project many years earlier when I took my first initial steps in the world of intellectual property rights and patents and found I missed having a book like this to help and guide me.

I am indeed indebted to a large number of people, several of whom should be singled out for special mention.

**Tim Frain**, for sparking my initial interest in the world of intellectual property and patents.

**Ilkka Rahnasto**, for giving me my initial opportunity to work on intellectual property matters and for trusting me to lead and manage Nokia's Patent Creation Factory.

**Sami Saru**, for his great help and support in getting the project off the ground.

**Jan Koeppen**, **Kevin Rivette**, **Ralph Eckardt**, **Harri Andersson** and **Tommi Kainu**, for opening my eyes to the possibilities.

**Amy Dixon** and **Morgan West**, for their motivation, dedication and sense of humour as student researchers on the project. The quality of their work was first class. I could not have completed this project without them.

**John O'Connell**, **John Samuels**, **Ian Johnson and Irene Bentley** for reviewing various early drafts, challenging me, making suggestions and urging me forward.

**Yrjo Neuvo**, **Urho Ilmonen**, **Lucy Nichols**, **Paul Melin**, **Sisko Piekkola**, **Thomas Wünnemann**, **Christian Bunke**, **Mark Cordy**, **Charles Bailey**, **Jay Erstling**, **Aino Metcalfe**, **Guy Gusnell**, **Bradley C. Wright**, **Shaun Sibley** and **Anu Chandra**, for giving me the positive encouragement to really get started on the book project when I only had the basic concept in place. Their initial feedback on the book concept was most appreciated way back then and motivated me to move forward in earnest.

**Anne Ruippo**, **Barbara Lindley**, **Kelly Wilcox** and **Nick Filler**, for sharing some of their knowledge and wisdom with me in the broader area of supplier and vendor management.

**Harri Poyhonen, Mikko Lintunen, Kari Syrjarinne** and **Heikki Korkeamaki**, for the insight and reference material they provided on the subject of innovation and creativity.

**Sue Harvey**, for looking after me throughout the duration of this project, reviewing drafts plus organising, helping and supporting me in so many different ways. A very special thank you for the major contribution she made to this book.

**Yrjo Neuvo, Anne Ruippo, John Samuels, John O'Connell, Sami Saru, Urho Ilmonen, Mika Lehtinen, Nick Filler, Timo Ruikka, Trevor Dragwidge** and **Ulla James**, for reviewing the complete draft versions of the book and for providing excellent constructive feedback.

**Anil Sinha, Omar Shoukry, Catherine Calais Regnier, Christine Wren, Mick Ralph, Vicente Aceituno, Kate Watkins, Professor Markus Reitzig, Dr Berthold Rutz** and **Guy Carmichael**, for providing formal permissions that allowed me to re-use some copyrighted material in the book. Thank you for being so kind and responsive to my requests for help and assistance on this matter.

**Marian Underweiser, Manny Schecter, Professor Beth Noveck** and **Professor Ronald Mann** for providing me with excellent insight into the workings of various patent quality initiatives. Thank you for being so helpful on this matter.

**Viv Wickham, Francesca Warren, Jo Golesworthy, Karen Weller, Natalie Garach** and **Michaela Fay**, from John Wiley & Sons, for guiding me painlessly through the publishing process.

**Liza and Shane O'Connell** for their love and support, especially for those times when I was working at home on the book, interrupting our precious family time together.

# 1
# Introduction

## Introduction

If one were challenged to think about a factory, production site or plant, one would typically picture a physical entity with components and raw material being delivered in and finished goods being shipped out.

The concept of a factory may be based on the large cotton mills in England in the 1800s, Henry Ford and his innovation with mass production in the early 20th century or today's mass customisation factories.

Inside this building, one can imagine production lines full of products, tools and test equipment. The building is busy with various activities taking place such as sorting, assembly, testing and packaging, with some of these activities being handled automatically while others are handled manually.

Now imagine walking into a large modern mass customisation factory where the material coming in one side of the factory consists not of physical components or raw materials but rather ideas, thoughts, inventions and solutions to problems, while patent applications or granted patents flow out the other side of the factory as the finished goods.

> *"Asset value isn't going to be found in machinery and equipment, warehouses or real estate – it's going to be found in patent portfolios."* Eric Gillespie, Advancing innovations as assets in the global marketplace. *FORTUNE Magazine Innovation Forum*, 5 December, 2005

This analogy linking modern factories and patent production is useful for a number of reasons. It is clear that the importance of intangible assets is growing, often equalling or surpassing the value of physical assets for a company. The state of the intellectual property of a company determines its share and corresponding influence on the market. The size and quality of its portfolio has a direct impact on several factors, such as the reputation of the company, the level of returns on investments and the access to the market, amongst others.

The way a company is valued has also changed considerably. In the mid-1970s, approximately 80% of the value of a company was made up of tangible assets, with the remaining 20% being made up of intangible assets. Today this percentage is completely reversed, with intangible assets making up 80% of the value of the company and only 20% being made up of tangible assets.

> *"Intellectual capital is recognised as the most important asset of many of the world's largest and most powerful companies; it is the foundation of the market dominance and continuing profitability of leading corporations."* Kelvin King, founding partner of Valuation Consulting

The volume of patent applications and granted patents has been increasing in recent years. As companies begin to realise the importance of intellectual property rights (IPR) in the modern business environment, it is unsurprising that this pattern has emerged. Indeed, companies are afraid that failure to evolve in correspondence with today's business climate will result in their competitors dominating the market in future.

The World Intellectual Property Office (WIPO) Patent Report, 2007 Edition (available at http://www.wipo.int/ipstats/en/statistics/patents/patent_report_2007.html), shows that worldwide filings of patent applications have grown at an average annual rate of 4.7%, with the highest growth rates experienced in North East Asian countries, particularly Korea and China. The report is based on 2005 figures and shows that patents granted worldwide have increased at an average annual rate of 3.6% with some 600000 patents granted in 2005 alone. By the end of 2005, approximately 5.6 million patents were in force worldwide.

The largest recipients of patent filings are the patent offices of Japan, the USA, China, Korea and the European Patent Office

(EPO). These five offices account for 77 % of all patents filed in 2005 (a 2 % increase over 2004) and represent 74 % of all patents granted. With an increase of almost 33 % over 2004, the patent office of China became the third largest recipient of patent filings in 2005.

Use of the international patent system has increased markedly in recent years and although it remains highly concentrated, with 49 % of the estimated 5.6 million patents in force being owned by applicants from Japan and the USA, there is evidence of an increase in the use of the system by newly industrialising nations.

However, the patenting process is by no means simple and there are various steps or stages in the process. The patenting language and terminology is often not easily understood and can also be a relatively expensive exercise. The reason for such complexity, in particular in the application and granting stages, is to ensure that the patents that do get through are of the utmost quality and provide protection only to the extent necessary.

Therefore, in today's highly competitive environment it is essential that we take a detailed look at how we go about producing these patents.

If one is concerned only with a few patents, one can probably stay with the individual handcrafted approach. However, as volumes increase it is better to compare and contrast how such patent creation activities are organised and structured to today's mass customisation operations and logistics, in order to then create and manage a patent portfolio.

> *"Leaders must encourage their organisations to dance to forms of music yet to be heard."*  Warren G. Bennis

This book is about the successful management and leadership of a patent factory and considers the organisational structure and mode of operation required. This involves providing clear direction and meaningful vision to all parts of an organisation, and deploying and controlling resources, be they people, money, and physical or intangible assets. Drawing from my experience and insights, this book guides readers along the path, providing advice about how best to arrange the human resources available to optimise the effectiveness and efficiency of the organisation. It then looks at which tasks are best conducted internally as opposed to outsourcing and what sort of organisation structures and formats work best. Decisions then need to be made on the key processes and the necessary tools to put in place.

This book highlights the key issues for consideration, the options available, the decision-making process and the opportunities and challenges that exist at each stage of this journey towards setting up a successful patent factory. In order to embark upon this journey you must ensure that you have the passion, determination and persistence in order to create a successful organisation.

Throughout this book, I will refer to this factory as a Patent Creation Factory.

# Why 'Inside the Patent Factory'?

The title of the book 'Inside the Patent Factory' obviously comes from the analogy painted above.

The factory analogy stems from the idea that patent creation should not be seen as some simple legal process but rather that it should be seen as a core activity of 'creating' patents, just like a factory creating products.

The basic idea is that if you wish to create patents as effectively as possible, you should then see the process like a factory production line, in which the end result is the granted patent. You should treat patent creation in much the same way that you would handle product development and granted patents just as you would handle a finished product.

However, it is important to realise that just as with modern factories, not all the tasks and activities are handled internally by the factory's own employees or even by the key suppliers and component vendors. Some tasks are outsourced to specialists.

> *"Companies are now treating intellectual property as a business asset not very different from a product on a shelf."* Ken Cukier, The Patent Survey, *The Economist*, Oct 2005

In this book, I will look at a number of critical success factors for this patent factory, starting with the overall goals and objectives of the factory followed by the organisational structure and mode of operation. Cost and quality management, internal versus outsourced activities and the flow of raw materials into the factory are all vital elements to consider.

## What questions does the book intend to answer?

I examine the key issues that any organisation interested in creating patents should consider and what options are available in terms of organisational structure and mode of operation. What are the factors to consider when making fundamental decisions about how to organise, structure and operate an organisation to create patents? I also look at some of the challenges that are likely to be faced along the way, such as deciding upon the correct metrics to use when managing and leading an organisation to create patents.

## Who is the target audience for this book?

This book should be of use to anyone interested in IPR, more specifically those interested in how to organise and structure people and processes to ensure that the patent creation part operates effectively and efficiently. As I myself researched and drafted this book, I reached out to many people from different backgrounds and experiences and not just those linked directly to Patent Creation Factory type activities. I found surprisingly strong interest in this subject matter across a quite diverse group of individuals, including the following:

- company managers interested in IPR and patent creation;

- IPR professionals within companies;

- External Patent Agencies filing and prosecuting cases on behalf of a Patent Creation Factory;

- functional managers with links to patent creation such as Human Resources, Finance and Quality;

- those involved in corporate strategy and strategy development;

- research and development managers interested in the subject of IPR and patents;

- investors interested in the intangible assets of companies;

- merger and acquisitions experts interested in the intangible assets of companies;

- the inventor community;

- students of business management;

- students of law and especially of IPR and patents.

Readers will gain a sound and detailed understanding of the workings of a Patent Creation Factory and its immediate environment. I describe everything from the point of view of a layperson so that the often confusing intellectual property concepts begin to appear relatively clear. Quotations from reputable sources are used to emphasise the significance of the text and case studies are provided to highlight specific issues. Moreover, analogies are used where it is felt that readers may struggle on first glance to come to terms with certain aspects. Ultimately, you need look no further to find a clear, yet detailed, account concerning the 'ins and outs' of what I term the Patent Creation Factory.

# Why have I written this book?

This book is based on my own experiences of managing and leading one such Patent Creation Factory and taking it through some dramatic organisational changes, including the removal of the matrix structure, a shift from site to technology focus, putting External Patent Agency management in place and conducting a major benchmarking exercise.

My primary responsibility has been in the management and leadership of a Patent Creation Factory.

I spent time and energy examining our organisational structure and mode of operation, reviewing various options and benchmarking our organisation against other companies and IPR organisations. I have also examined the interface to other parts of IPR, to the inventor community, to External Patent Agencies and to other parts of the company.

I very much wish to document what I have gained from these experiences and to share my learning and insight with those who may find it beneficial. I have also read many IPR books already published but believe that few, if any, concentrate on the organisational structure and mode of operation of the Patent Creation part of IPR.

Encouragement to write this book came from discussions with many IPR professionals and business and technology managers, because many are thinking about how to restructure or reorganise their IPR departments but do not know how. Therefore, there is a clear need for the book.

IPR is becoming more and more important to a company's success and it is crucial that the patent creation part of IPR is well organised and has an efficient and effective mode of operation.

There are still some things to learn about how best to manage and lead a Patent Creation Factory and I will continue to learn and develop and no doubt make some mistakes along the way. I hope that the writing of this book marks a key milestone on my learning journey and that this book also helps readers as they progress along their own learning journey.

## Patent creation explained

The word 'creation' is very meaningful in this context because the basic idea is to really 'create' patents, as opposed to just drafting legal documents and filing them to relevant patent offices. Patent creation should not be seen as a bureaucratic activity, concerned only with the formalities of the process, but as much more than this: it should be suitably elevated to the role of a 'factory' at the heart of a company's IPR activities.

Patent creation is the activity within IPR that involves interfacing to the inventor community, gathering inventions, analysing them, making decisions and then filing and prosecuting cases. It can be seen as a virtual factory, producing quality patents at the end of the production line for others in IPR to utilise.

However, it is not an isolated factory disconnected from the rest of IPR and the company or the business environment, it is a factory well connected to those developing strategies. Actively linked to the inventor community, it takes pride in raising awareness of IPR throughout the company and continuously grows and develops its people, processes and tools. Furthermore, it does the basics well, such as harvesting inventions, reviewing those inventions and filing and prosecuting those considered of value, ultimately to obtain good quality granted patents.

The leader and manager of this Patent Creation Factory formulates a long-term strategy for the factory on the basis of the overall IPR strategy and the overall company strategy. This person then identifies competencies needed to achieve the strategic objectives and targets and ensures team and individual targets are in line with the strategic objectives of the factory. He or she actively monitors the source, volume and quality of the raw material (inventions) coming into the factory and participates in factory process and tool development, while managing the budget in a professional business manner. This process will ultimately ensure the quality of the patents produced within the factory.

Patent creation clearly involves an array of activities that you need to be aware of with the overall objective being to create good quality patents, hence the term 'patent creation'.

# Multiple regimes of intellectual property protection

It is most important to realise that multiple regimes of intellectual property protection exist. Although this book concentrates solely on patents and not on other elements of IPR such as trademarks, designs, domain names, copyright, etc., these other rights remain important and warrant some definition (see Table 1.1). It is also important to take a holistic view of IPR, and to realise that the premeditated use of multiple intellectual property regimes can help achieve sustainable differentiation.

These rights differ substantially in many ways, and the rules applicable are different. It is therefore not fitting for them to be discussed here as many other books are available on these other rights. However, what must be kept in mind is that patents are just one of the many rights that exist to protect intangible assets and thus IPR, more than ever before, is essential in today's market economy.

> *"If this business were split up, I would give you the land and bricks and mortar, and I would take the brands and trade marks, and I would fare better than you."* John Stuart, Chairman of Quaker (c. 1900)

**Table 1.1**  The multiple regimes of intellectual property rights

| | |
|---|---|
| **Patents** | A patent protects an invention. It gives the holder an exclusive right to prevent others from selling, making and using the patented invention for a certain period (typically 20 years from filing date). |
| **Copyright** | Copyright protects the expression of literary or artistic work. Protection arises automatically giving the holder the exclusive right to control reproduction or adaptation. |
| **Trademarks** | A trademark is a distinctive sign that is used to distinguish the products or services of one business from others. A trademark is closely linked to brand. |
| **Design** | The design protects the form of appearance, style or design of an object. It does not protect the functionality. |
| **Utility models** | A utility model is an intellectual property right to protect inventions. This right is available in a number of national legislations. It is very similar to the patent, but usually has a shorter term (often 6 or 10 years) and less stringent patentability requirements. |
| **Semi-conductor topography ('silicone chips')** | This protects two or three-dimensional layout or topography of an integrated circuit. It is somewhat similar to copyright. |
| **Database rights** | Database right prevents copying of substantial parts of a database. However, unlike copyright the protection is not over the form of expression of information but of the information itself. In many other respects, database right is similar to copyright. |
| **Trade secrets** | A trade secret is a formula, practice, process, design, instrument, pattern or compilation of information used by a business to obtain an advantage over competitors or customers. Trade secrets are by definition *not* disclosed to the world at large. |

# A somewhat unique factory

This chapter sets the scene of the book. If you wish to have patenting activities, you should consider how to create patents effectively and efficiently by forming a Patent Creation Factory.

However, although the analogy of a factory explains the patent creation process, one must appreciate the unique nature of patents and the inevitable exceptions that come with applying such an analogy. Some aspects of the factory analogy may not be so obvious to some readers, or may indeed even cause confusion, and so I clarify below a few aspects of the analogy.

- Patents can cover a wide range of topics and each patent is different, whereas a factory often produces the same product repeatedly. The goal of most factories is to increase production while lowering costs. However, a patent factory must foster innovation and quality should almost certainly be more important than quantity.

- Factories can be automated (the same inputs at one end produce the same outputs at the other), but with patents, if you take the same set of ideas, expertise and knowledge you do not necessarily get the same patents as output.

- The patent process must also tolerate 'rejects'. Not every idea will become a valuable patent; some ideas may already have been patented, others may not be sufficiently original, etc. In contrast, factories are measured on their efficiency, with the aim of eliminating all waste (i.e., no faulty products) and by constantly testing and measuring the output from the production line.

Overall, the concept of a patent factory accurately portrays the need for an effective and efficient procedure in order to maximise a company or organisations gain when creating a patent or more importantly building a patent portfolio.

# The structure of the book

The book begins by stressing the need for a strategic plan to help direct the long-term operation of the Patent Creation Factory. It then addresses some basic fundamentals that are key to the success of any such factory, namely understanding why patents can be of importance and of value to you, an appreciation of innovation and the need to harvest inventions, and the need to know the ins and outs of the actual patenting process. The book then moves to discussing in depth the key external interfaces such as the inventor community, senior management, the External Patent Agencies and so forth, as no factory can work in isolation. Various organisational models and modes of operation for the Patent Creation Factory are then examined with specific detailed information supplied on the management of the relationship with External Patent Agencies. This is followed by a number of chapters related to metrics, with special emphasis on quality and costs. Factory processes and tools are then discussed, before the book prompts the reader to look outside the factory, using benchmarking against others as well as examining major changes taking place in the patent world.

# 2
# Building a strategy

## Introduction

This chapter invites you to consider your own patent needs
and asks some key questions to prompt you to initiate or
further develop your strategy relating to patent creation. I
want to force you to think about your own needs, your
current situation regarding intellectual property and what
you want your patent portfolio to be like in the future.
Key questions relating to strategy, objectives and aims
are asked in order to help you to create and improve a
patent creation strategy. The questions guide you through
the subject and provide answers and examples along the
way about the theory of strategy and how it is critical
to intellectual property, and how to develop a strategy as
well the key themes and issues involved. When dealing
with intellectual property and patent creation management, it is critical to think strategically about this subject
matter.

> *"2006 marks the first year of the 11th Chinese five-year plan. The focus of this plan is to foster independent innovation and build an innovation-oriented country. Intellectual property (IP) rights form a central plank in this transition from a manufacturing to innovation-based economy."* From "World Economic Forum on China Business Summit 2006"

To ensure that your intellectual property strategy is an excellent strategy in the future, the book will give you exemplary questions and hints to help you analyse your current situation and to see and predict possible changes happening in the future with your business environment. I invite you to consider some key questions that are relevant when creating, implementing and further developing an intellectual property strategy and I will guide and assist you to create and shape your intellectual property strategy to be aligned with the overall company strategy. The purpose of this chapter is to ask if you know where you are and where you want to be in the future and it should prompt you to think about strategic issues.

## Strategy explained

> *"Strategy is a plan you adopt in order to get something done."* Collins Cobuild English Language Dictionary

One may think that strategy is something theoretical or impractical, but in general this is not the case and it is certainly not the case with intellectual property. Just like in a factory, there needs to be a plan that is followed when deciding what to produce and when. Similarly, every company should have a plan for the company's activities and this should always include intellectual property activities.

Every strategy is, and should be, unique and different, since business needs, business environments and company resources and targets are also unique. Good strategy takes into account the current situation and the needs and targets, but it should be especially created to ensure that the company can be successful in the future and in a changing environment.

> *"The essence of strategy is choosing to perform activities differently than rivals do . . . a company can out perform rivals only if it can establish a difference that it can preserve."* From Michael Porter's *What is Strategy*

It is critical that one thinks strategically when dealing with intellectual property and patent creation management, because patent creation cannot operate in tactical short-term mode. A strategy is a long-term plan designed to achieve a particular objective or level of success. Strategy differs from tactical planning or immediate actions with resources at hand. It was originally associated with military matters, but the word strategy has become commonly used in many fields, for example business and corporate strategy.

When talking about strategy, it is worth clarifying some of the phrases and terms often used (Table 2.1).

**Table 2.1** Phrases and terms used in strategy creation

| | |
|---|---|
| Vision | Paints a clear picture of your environment at the end of your strategic time frame |
| Current state | Defines your position in terms of strengths, weaknesses, opportunities and threats at the present time |
| Strategy | Your long-term plan of campaign to achieve a particular goal or objective |
| Mission statement | Defines how this plan will be achieved |
| Strategic intent | Defines where you wish to be at the end of the strategic time period |
| Strategic actions | Defines the top level actions you plan to take, in order to move from where you are today to where you wish to be at the end of your strategic time frame |
| Strategic reviews | Defines how you plan to review your progress as you move along |
| Metrics | Defines the measures you plan to put in place to monitor your progress |
| Values | Defines the culture and mode of behaviour |

For a more expansive explanation on strategy, I refer you to the book *The Art of War*. Although this is an ancient military handbook, it is in such an environment that the origins of strategy can be found. In the 6th century BC, Sun Tzu wrote this classic book of military strategy based on Chinese warfare and military thought. It is one of the oldest books on military strategy in the world and had a huge influence on Eastern and Western military thinking, business tactics and beyond. Like a work of science, much of the book is dedicated to explaining its concepts as a series of formulas.

Sun Tzu was the first to recognise the importance of position-ing in strategy and that position is affected both by objective conditions in the physical environment plus the subjective opinions of competitors in that environment. He taught that strategy was not planning in the sense of working through a to-do list, but instead it requires appropriate, quick responses to changing conditions. Planning works best in a controlled environment, but in a competitive environment you will find that competing plans collide, therefore creating situations that no one can foresee.

# Getting started

There are many approaches to strategic planning but typically a three-phase approach may be taken:

- **Current state:** an analysis of where you are today and how it came about.

- **Ideal state:** a clearly defined statement of intent stating where you wish to be at the end of the strategic period.

- **Strategic actions:** a course to plot on how to get from where you are today to where you wish to be at the end of the strategic time period.

When developing strategies, an analysis of the current state, such as the organisation structure, mode of operation, skills and competencies is needed, as well as its processes and tools, financial situation and environment. Customer focus is also very important. The analysis has to be conducted in an honest and thorough fashion so as to identify strengths, weaknesses, opportunities and threats.

The ideal state may sometimes be defined by means of a mission statement or a vision statement, but it is important that these two statements should not be confused with one another as many people mistake a vision statement for a mission statement. A vision statement should describe the future identity, whereas a mission statement should describe how that identity is to be achieved. A mission statement may further define the purpose or broader goal for being in existence or in business and it serves as an ongoing guide without a time frame. The mission statement, if crafted well, can remain the same for many years! Vision is more specific in terms of an objective and future state and the vision is related to some form of achievement if successful.

Plotting a course from where you are today to where you wish to be at the end of the strategic time period involves taking a number of steps.

## Format of a strategy

Although there is no defined look and feel to a strategy or a strategy document, it may be useful to define a template to help Patent Creation Factory management with the creation of this type of long-term plan. I have found the format shown in Table 2.2 to be useful.

A battle cry here should be somewhat similar to the yell or slogan taken up in battle. This battle cry can serve many purposes, including inspiring others who may be inclined to stay back and also to promote a sense of togetherness and common purpose. The rules of engagement determine

**Table 2.2** Format of a strategy

Battle Cry or Mission Statement

Rules of engagement, constraints, limitations

Top level objectives

Top level action plans

Strategic roadmap or time-line

Foundations or cornerstones of your strategy

SWOT Analysis

Metrics

Review process

Team level goals

Individual goals

when, where and how your actions can be conducted, and it is worthwhile specifying these precisely so that everyone involved knows the limitations imposed and the constraints that are in place. Strategic planning and decision processes should then lead to objectives and a roadmap of ways to achieve those objectives. SWOT Analysis is a strategic planning tool that can be used to evaluate the Strengths, Weaknesses, Opportunities and Threats involved in an activity such as a project or a business venture. It involves specifying the objective of the activity and identifying the factors, both internal and external, that are favourable and unfavourable to achieving that objective. Metrics enable calculations and comparisons to be made in order to establish whether everything is running with targets. You must carry out ongoing monitoring of your strategy to manage it effectively and make sure that it is a dynamic process and not a stagnant document.

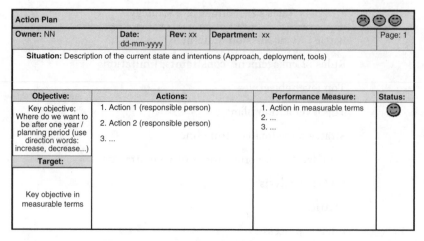

**Figure 2.1**   Template for an action plan.

The template shown in Figure 2.1 may help as you set about creating and managing your action plans.

# Developing a strategy

> *"In the past two years, the company has reshaped its entire strategy around innovation and patents."*
> Microsoft

To get started, a number of key questions need to be asked and answered:

- Why do you want to patent your inventions?

- What is your business about today and in the future?

- How is the intellectual property game played in your industry? What are the formal and informal rules of this game and will the rules change? Will there be new players?

- What is the current state of your own patent portfolio?

- Where do you want to be?

Several benefits come with patenting your inventions. Perhaps the most obvious is that a patent grants an exclusive right to manufacture, use and sell the patented invention for a period of up to 20 years. This provides a competitive edge over your competitors. Another benefit that flows from patenting is the positive image attached to both your company and the invention itself, inasmuch as you are seen as forward-looking and innovative. This may in turn increase profits and attract investment to cover the initial research and development costs, as well as any future costs in the further development of the invention. Also, if you do not have the resources, be that the capital to exploit the invention or the technology to produce it, patenting the invention provides the necessary protection against 'imitators', as well as the ability to license out to others who are in possession of the necessary resources. This protection inevitably extends to those who do have the resources but have found others infringing their exclusive right. Finally, by patenting your invention you avoid the scenario in which you find a competitor has chosen to patent the invention before you, and consequently, avoid finding yourself wrapped up in costly litigation.

The benefits associated with patenting need to be weighed against the relevant costs and the financial considerations, including agent fees, administrative charges, renewal fees and possibly the costs of translation. Make no mistake; taking out a patent is not cheap. The time and effort required in drafting the patent application, the application procedure and also the maintenance of the invention must be taken into account. A factor often taken for granted but that must be remembered, is that the applicant must make its invention available to the public when patenting an invention. This often provides competitors with sufficient information to 'invent around' the patent.

The first question that needs to be answered before you embark on creating your strategy is why you want to patent your inventions and indeed, by weighing up the costs and benefits, it may become clearer which route to take. Patenting may or may not be the best route for your inventions or market. Moreover, the motivation behind seeking a patent will play a key role in shaping your strategy.

To understand your business fully, you need to ask and answer these types of questions:

- How is technology changing?

- How is the competition changing in your industry and how is the business model and way of doing business changing?

- What are the major disruptions coming in your industry?

- What are the weak signals, and is anything just beyond the horizon that may change things in the future?

- What legal or regulatory changes might affect your industry and how could the likes, dislikes, trends and fashion of end-users influence your industry?

It is also important that you really know and understand the strength and weaknesses of your current patent portfolio:

- What is the volume of your patent portfolio?

- What is the quality of your patent portfolio and how is it growing and developing?

- How is it being trimmed?

- What competitive intelligence do you have and how does your portfolio stand up when compared and contrasted to others (competitors, suppliers, customers)?

- How are these others utilising their patents compared to you?

- Do you know where your patents apply per jurisdiction?

Where do you *want* to be at the end of your strategy time period and where do you *need* to be at the end of your strategic time period in order to be successful? Although patents last for 20 years, setting short-term targets gives you something to aim for and acts as a benchmark for you to assess your strategy and judge it as either a failure or a success. Target setting also helps you break down the process into several parts, which in turn helps you allocate your time and resources more efficiently.

Finally, how do you intend to exploit your patent? Although this aspect is part of the larger intellectual property strategy, rather than the Patent Creation Factory strategy, these two strategies must be in alignment. It is also critical that there is alignment between your overall intellectual property strategy and your company strategy, particularly in such areas as innovation and new business activities.

## Validate and test your strategy

A number of simple questions have to be asked to test the strategy, such as how good is the market research or other information upon which the strategic plan is founded? Have you defined the end states (objectives) correctly and how honest and thorough has the SWOT analysis been conducted with respect to the desired end state(s)? You also need to ask if there has been good creativity and innovation shown when identifying possible strategies: is the strategic action plan capable of achieving the desired objective and is the strategic action plan feasible? You need to determine whether the estimation of resources, skills and competencies, and of time, personnel or financial requirements, is realistic. Is there a good coordination process in place? Finally, are there effective attempts to gain the support of others or address areas of resistance taking place and are the mechanisms in place to ensure that the project plan will be followed, reviewed and adjusted if necessary. There needs to be excellent senior management in place, combined with a good leadership focus and sponsorship.

# The characteristics of a good strategy

It is best if the strategy you create is relatively clear and straightforward because this increases the chance of successful implementation. An overcomplicated strategy is prone to be misunderstood or misconstrued at a later date. The best strategies are those that only deal with the most important issues; anything unessential to the overall plan should be left to your discretion when the decision must be made. That way you can stay focused on your overall goals while assessing the market environment there and then. This helps to keep your strategy fresh and you are more likely to stick to it. An overcomplicated strategy may prove too rigid and therefore detrimental to your ultimate target, so you will always need to build in some flexibility. You should ideally be able to convey a summary of your strategy in the time it takes the lift in your company headquarters to go from ground level up to the top floor.

The strategy and top-level action plan needs to cascade down to individual level, this way everyone knows what they are doing. Although it is important to keep your strategy as simple as possible, you should not skimp on the attention to detail, because this can essentially decide whether your strategy is successful or not. By ensuring that everyone is in the loop as to their roles and responsibilities, focus is maintained and everyone will work more efficiently in producing the targeted result.

The strategy for the Patent Creation Factory needs to be in alignment with the overall intellectual property strategy and the overall company strategy. Incompatible strategies send out mixed messages and the end result will inevitably be a strategy that does not go hand in hand with what the other key areas of your business are doing. An aligned company strategy sends out signals that your company is unified and ultimately competent. Once developed, the strategy needs to be communicated to the organisation and possibly beyond, to the likes of Senior Management, Business and Technology Management, the other half of intellectual property, External Patent Agencies and the inventor community. This is in order to ensure that everyone is aware and in unison.

You may also wish to consider promoting the creation of a public version of your intellectual property strategy. You may wish to demonstrate the benefits that your inventions are bringing to society as well as the respect you have for intellectual property rights belonging to others (see the following panel).

---

### Nokia's Patent Creation Factory Strategy

Nokia has been very successful with its strategy because a strong focus on innovation and technological advancement has always been on its strategic agenda. The company emphasises the importance of promoting a 'passion for innovation' among the workers and considers it a vital value within the company.

Nokia recognises the increasing importance attached to continuously making leading edge innovations. These inventions support its competitive strategic business goals in a number of different ways, one of which is an application for patent protection over selected technological inventions. However, Nokia's approach is to use patenting selectively while screening applications after the initial patenting decision. Since 1998, Nokia has filed around 1000 new patent applications each year, with each new patent costing a cumulative patent cost of approximately £70 000 (€100 000) spread over a 20-year period. Patenting is therefore a fairly expensive means of protection and with a portfolio the size of Nokia's you are looking at a major investment, which requires adjustment on a global scale against business measures such as operating profit and R&D cost. As an intellectual property function, Nokia needs to be able to either clearly show a return on investment for each technology area, where it wants to invest, or make a clear proposal for reserving certain portions of the overall budget for risk investments.

As an example, it may be that it is adequate to have 10 good patents in a specific technology area, because filing more patents will not bring an adequate return on investment. However, if Nokia wants to protect its differentiation features, it may choose to consider which new features will bring real value. The patenting decision needs to be based on such a judgment. Another factor to consider is whether the intellectual property licences in certain technologies are more or less in place already. When completely new technologies or standards are created, and the intellectual property environment in that standard is not known, Nokia may find it justifiable to try to file almost as many patent applications as possible in order to ensure its competitive advantage in any impending licensing negotiations.

Annually, Nokia intellectual property is enhancing its planning capabilities in order to ensure that its investment in patenting is optimised from its business viewpoint. At the same time, Nokia's intellectual property is seeking to encourage all new innovations. The company wants to promote active dialogue with inventors, when the inventors feel that the intellectual property has not fully captured the potential of their inventions.

There are various ways of extracting value out of inventions that are not patented, such as keeping them as trade secrets or publicising them. Nokia uses a web site to publish inventions that it does not intend to patent. This strategy acts as both a channel to publish high quality research results, as well as a source of protection should the same invention be later patented by another party.

# Monitoring and reviewing your strategy

Continually reviewing your strategy is vital. Companies face continual change and your strategy must respond, because an inflexible strategy is a failed one. If possible, while planning your initial strategy, try to prepare alternative routes based on the different outcomes of a predicted variable. This can leave you in good stead because all that needs doing is for that route to be followed. However, this is only a possibility where such variables are limited and foreseeable. When it is not possible to draw up a contingency plan, continually monitoring and updating your strategy is essential in order for it to remain relevant, focused and ultimately successful.

You must set up processes for reviewing objectives, targets and action plans and carry out ongoing monitoring of your strategy in order to manage it effectively and make sure that it become_ _ _ _ ng and dynamic process.

Your strateg_ _ _ _ be marketed as a key document to everyone involved _ _ o it often and use it as the basis for performance m_ _ _ _ . Your strategy should also reflect the approach you are _ _ _ _ with regard to monitoring.

It is essential that yo_ _op action plans for each priority area in your strategy to make sure implementation is realistic. This will in turn provide a basis for ongoing monitoring and evaluation, which is essential if you are to turn your strategy into action and make sure that work is broken down into manageable chunks with interim targets and milestones.

Objectives and targets must be clear and mean something to those who are being asked to work towards achieving them. Baselines are a key part of monitoring and evaluation because they enable you to measure what your actions have achieved.

Performance measures are used to see whether inputs, outputs and outcomes are being achieved. Choose performance measures that support each other so that they can provide good evidence of the success or failure of a particular action. If your chosen performance measurement information is not readily available you should develop processes to collect it.

Make sure you know why you are monitoring and evaluating your key strategic action plans and have a clear idea of what you want to know as a result of this process. Use a model for evaluation to help plan your monitoring and evaluation processes.

Describe the monitoring and evaluation processes in your strategy document, including how often monitoring/evaluation will take place, and details of who is responsible for collecting and analysing the monitoring information. Also include the format in which the information will be presented, to whom the information will be presented for comment/action and how the findings will inform the strategy review process.

You will need to have systems in place to monitor the progress regularly of your action plans at a strategic level, so that mitigating action can be taken to achieve your objective if the chosen action is not working. Monitoring progress against key milestones allows you to learn and do something different if what you are doing is not producing the desired results.

## Summary

There is a wealth of extremely useful and well-written literature available on the subject of strategy. I have highlighted a few key issues associated with strategy in this chapter but I strongly recommend that you read some reputable books on the subject of strategy as your first step in creating an efficient and effective Patent Creation Factory.

> *"Strategy without tactics is the slowest route to victory. Tactics without strategy is the noise before defeat."* Sun Tzu

My own approach is to break down the task of creating a comprehensive winning strategy into manageable chunks. Understand your requirements and needs, including an analysis of your current state and your ideal end state, and then formulate and define your strategy. Follow this process by validating and testing your strategy, before you articulate, communicate and publish your strategy, so that everyone involved is well informed. Finally you must monitor and review progress with your strategy on a regular basis and adapt as necessary.

# 3
# Why patent?

## What is a patent?

In order to embark upon the journey of patent creation you must first understand patents and how they work. You must also understand and appreciate the rights and obligations that accompany patents, otherwise you will have no foundation upon which to build your 'patent factory'. It is essential to realise that patents and the patenting process are serious business.

> *"Patent protection is a central feature of the innovation process. It is crucial that inventors and businesses fully understand the whole patent system, for their own benefit and that of the economy."* Ron Marchant, the new Chief Executive of the UK Patent Office (May 2006) http://www.patent.gov.uk

A patent is an exclusive right granted for an invention. Patents are generally intended to cover products or processes that contain new functional or technical aspects. They are therefore concerned with how things work, what they do, how they do it, what they are made of or how they are made. Patent protection means that the invention cannot be commercially made, used, distributed or sold without the patent owner's consent. This protection is granted for a limited period, generally 20 years from filing.

The owner of a patent has the right to decide who may, or may not, use the patented invention. The patent owner may give permission to use the invention, or license other parties to use the invention, on mutually agreed terms. The owner may also sell the right to the invention to someone else, who then becomes the new owner of the patent.

The government grants patents – a limited property right – to inventors, in exchange for their agreement to share the details of their inventions with the public, in order to enrich the total body of technical knowledge in the world. This promotes further creativity and innovation in others and therefore benefits humans as technology constantly improves.

Patents provide incentives to individuals by offering them recognition for their creativity and potential reward for their marketable inventions.

These incentives encourage innovation and many large modern corporations have annual research and development (R&D) budgets. Without patent protection, R&D spending would be significantly less or eliminated altogether, limiting the possibility of technological advances or breakthroughs as third parties would be free to exploit any developments.

The exact statutory definition of a patent differs between different countries, but the principles outlined above are generally valid.

# A brief history of patents

Patent law is generally accepted to have started with the Venetian Statute of 1474, although patents themselves had been in existence before that date. The Republic of Florence issued a decree, which stated that all novel and inventive devices had to be communicated to the Republic in order to gain legal protection for a decade against any potential infringement.

## Patents in the UK

The first record of patents in the UK dates back to the reign of Henry VI. The crown would issue a 'letters patent', meaning open letters, which would provide someone with a monopoly to produce a particular good. The first recorded patent was awarded to a Flemish national in 1449 for a period of 20 years, protecting a glass-making process that at the time was unknown in England.

The crown used its ability to grant monopolies to raise money and, unsurprisingly, this power was abused as all sorts of common goods, such as salt, were granted patents. Consequently, the court became more reluctant to award patents and limited the circumstances that would enable them to be granted. James I of England was subsequently forced to revoke all existing patents and declare that they were only to be used for 'projects of new invention'. This was incorporated by Parliament into the Statute of Monopolies, which restricted the crown's power to the extent that patents could only be granted to inventors of original inventions for a fixed number of years.

The reign of Queen Anne (1702–14) saw lawyers of the English Court develop the requirement that for a patent to be granted, a written description of the invention must be submitted. These developments were the foundations of patent law in the US, New Zealand and Australia.

The Patents Act 1977 harmonised UK patent law with that in place in Europe. It was one of the most radical pieces of patent legislation to be passed for nearly a century and enabled the UK to join the European Patent Convention. This legislation replaced the Statute of Monopolies and is still in place today.

The 1980s witnessed the development of supra-national patent-issuing authorities such as the European Patent Office and the World Intellectual Property Office (WIPO). These bodies enabled patent applications to be filed in a number of countries simultaneously.

## Patents in the USA

The UK patent system acted as the foundation for the American system. Immigrants from England brought their system with them and as such many similarities can be seen, for example a concern for the rights of the inventor and society in general.

During the colonial period, states in the US had their own patent systems and it wasn't until 1790 that a national system was adopted by Congress in the form of a Patent Act. The US Constitution helped promote the necessary environment for scientists and inventors to protect and market their creations.

The Intellectual Property Clause of the US Constitution states that 'Congress shall have the power to promote the progress of science and useful arts by securing for limited times to authors and inventors the exclusive right to their respective writings and discoveries'. Although vague, this documents the duty of the government to protect the citizens' exclusive right to their intellectual property.

Following the ratification of the Constitution, several acts were passed by Congress to aid the development of a national patent system and the Patent Act of 1790 required all patent applications to be submitted with models. This followed Thomas Jefferson's belief that ideas should not be patentable, but rather that patents should only be issued for physical inventions, which had been essentially reduced to practice (see the 'Industrially applicable' section on p. 55). The Act also limited the life of a patent to 14 years with no possibility of extension and disqualified foreign imported patents, with only Americans being afforded the benefits of patent rights.

The 1793 Patent Act formally created a Patent Board comprising of the Secretary of State, Attorney General and Secretary of War. The Secretary of State was responsible for issuing the patent, providing that two-thirds of the board deemed the invention as being 'sufficiently useful and important'. Often the members of the board were not experts in the relevant field and as such many patents were granted that should not have been. Although the Act proved to have its own shortcomings it was introduced in response to complaints that its predecessor was inefficient, with applications taking months to be examined with only half of those received being examined during 1790–93. This inefficiency acted as a deterrent to inventors.

Between 1793 and 1836 the number of patent applications soared. This highlighted several problems for the still loosely organised patent office and as a result the quality of patents suffered, with many lacking novelty and usefulness. On top of this, the courts were overwhelmed by a large number of infringement and patent validity suits. To rectify this problem, Congress passed the Act of 1836 that established a separate Patent Office and this helped increase the efficiency of the application process. The Act also created a means for distributing new patents to libraries in every state. The aim of this was to provide the general public with access to knowledge disclosed within the various patents, so as to increase the number of new applications as well as enhance their quality. Furthermore, the Act also extended the life of a patent by providing for an extension period of an additional seven years. These changes helped create an environment in which individuals and business were able to exploit the marketplace to the fullest extent possible and the royalties paid made many people very wealthy.

The US Civil War and the period that followed led to a boom in the number of patents being issued in specialised areas. Many patents were related to military applications, for example, Gatling's machine gun patent, and the period leading up to and including World War I saw patents issued for a submarine, airplane, rocket and hydroplane. Similarly, patents issued during the era of World War II included the jet engine and atomic reactor.

Although the 18th and 19th centuries saw patents awarded only to physical inventions that were considered useful, the mid-20th century held a much more liberal attitude of patenting 'everything made under the sun'. More inventors led to more patents being filed! These included a Cotton Gin patent, a Morse Code patent, a Vulcanised Rubber patent and a Telephone patent. This explosion of patents enabled the rise of corporations, which helped America grow into an economic power.

The system created by the Patent Act of 1836 is still largely intact with a few minor adjustments. However, this system has led to continued abuses and problems with the US Patent Office, with patents currently taking several years from the date of filing to the date they are issued; often, a patent is issued after the technology has become obsolete. Patents are still being granted for obvious, non-useful inventions and there exists a flood of patent infringement litigation.

## Patents in Japan

The history of the patent system in Japan started with a 'law for new things' being passed in 1721. Prior to this there was a tendency to despise new things as Japan was ruled at this time by military commanders, who used to control the civilians by prohibiting any form of luxury. This required civilians to live in a modest manner and the 1721 law prohibited any form of inventing.

However, in 1868 the governmental power returned to the Emperor and it was soon realised that a patent system was a necessity if there was to be any attempt to modernise. Japanese delegates were sent to the US and Europe to negotiate free trade and learn about their political systems, industrial technologies and cultures. At this point in history, Europe was in the midst of the Industrial Revolution and patenting of new technologies was very popular. The Japanese delegates took this knowledge back with them and chose to base their new system on the policies of the European countries. The Patent Monopoly Act followed in 1885, which was mainly based on French Patent Law, but this only lasted a year: it was decided that the Japanese people did not understand it sufficiently after they protested, claiming that it took away their freedom to copy. Another factor was that the government office was experiencing problems with the application of the Monopoly Act.

In 1905 the utility model law was introduced to accommodate smaller inventions and in 1921 the basis of the current patent law was compiled. Since then a major amendment has been passed and issued in 1995 and this law is currently still in place.

## Patents elsewhere in the world

The majority of African or Latin American countries base their intellectual property systems on that of their colonial ancestors and although they may have tweaked the odd rule, the footprint can still be seen. For example, a closer inspection of the Nigerian system shows that it is heavily based on the UK system. However, although this may be the case for some states, not all countries are as developed, because private law is a luxury possessed only by the more developed of nations. States may not have the mechanisms in place to recognise intellectual property rights (IPR) and indeed an attitude exists whereby such rights are seen as a tool of the western world to restrict competition. Organisations such as WIPO exist to help change this perception and provide encouragement to developing nations to adopt their own systems, enabling them to recognise the rights of foreign inventors and also to protect the rights of those based in their own country. Until this is done, the full benefits of IPR will not flow down to the less developed of nations.

# Reasons to patent

The importance of intellectual property is finally being recognised as companies realise the significance of protecting their innovations. This can be seen in the growth of patent applications: a look at the patent portfolios of several major

companies over the past decade shows the increasing awareness of just how important intellectual property is now considered to be.

> *"The large picture here is that intellectual property is
> the crucial capital in a global knowledge economy."*
> Samuel J Palmisano, IBM Chief Executive. Source: New York Times
> Autumn 2006

Patents give clear proof of ownership, because a patent is
similar to a land certificate when you own a house and a patent
owner has the exclusive right to prevent others from the commercial use of their invention. This not only increases your
market share significantly, but also decreases the uncertainty
and risk that are inherent with imitators and free-riders. If
your company owns or obtains permission to exploit a patented invention, you are more likely to become a pre-eminent
player in the relevant market.

> *"If you didn't have patents, you would be in a very
> disadvantaged position relative to your competitors."*
> Liuping Song, the head of Huawei's Intellectual Property Depart-
> ment, in Shenzen

An invention may have required a huge investment in time
and money while the research and development was performed. Patent protection aids in the recovery of these costs
and helps obtain higher returns on that investment than
otherwise might have been expected.

As a patent owner you may not want to give up what has the potential to be a lucrative invention, however, for one reason or another, you may not have the necessary resources to exploit it. Through licensing your rights to others, in exchange for a payment or royalties, you may gain a steady income without the costs, risks and uncertainties of exploitation.

If you own the patent but do not possess the technology needed to exploit it, you may wish to negotiate a cross-licensing agreement, whereby you permit another company to use your patent in exchange for the provision of the necessary technology.

Licensing your patent to another may provide access to a new market, which may otherwise have been inaccessible.

Patenting your invention prevents others from patenting the same or similar inventions. Not only does it give your company a competitive edge, but it also reduces the probability that you may infringe the rights of others when commercialising your invention.

> *"We have to constantly conduct systematic innovation or else we will be eliminated by the competition."*
> Chen Tonghai Chairman, China Petroleum & Chemical Corporation (Sinopec) People's Republic of China

A patent portfolio separates you from the crowd. It demonstrates a high level of professionalism, expertise and innovation, as well as the technological capacity of your company. It will undoubtedly have a positive effect, creating business, increasing your profile and raising funds amongst other things.

> *"We need to increase the development of our independently owned technologies."* Cheng Siwei Vice-Chairman, Standing Committee, National People's Congress, People's Republic of China

Patents are published typically 18 months after the first filing date so that we can all learn about the technology and the associated information is easily searchable and freely available online. Without patents and the publication of patents, it is more than likely that many new system technologies would remain secret. Although perhaps not top of a company's agenda, the publishing of patents also provides greater knowledge to others. Patented inventions are easy to search for over the Internet and subsequently people can learn about the idea behind the technology and potentially look to advance it. This process is called 'inventing around', as one can use the information of a previously patented invention to come up with another invention that may be patentable. Despite not being in the best interests of the company who patented the invention, releasing information that may prove useful to competitors is seen as necessary in order to encourage innovation, as well as to prevent a system of secrecy.

Patents are not solely of benefit to established enterprises but also bring benefits to start-ups. As well as providing protection for new business ventures, a patent opens the door and allows for discussions with potential partners, customers, suppliers and competitors, and provides a level playing field for all the stakeholders involved.

Patents help the process of open standardisation as they encourage investment in innovation. This is also true for interoperability standards. Filing a patent application allows technology developers to disclose and share their ideas openly and early and this in turn enables technical specifications to be promulgated consensually for the benefit of the industry. These specifications may, and probably will, include patented technology. Without patents, the approach taken by many would be to keep things secret. Organisations that set standards recognise the contribution made by patents, and they have intellectual property policies in place. These policies are there to strike a balance between the rights of the patent holder to enjoy the full benefits of the patent, the rights of third parties to make and sell interoperating products and last but not least the right of the public to benefit from the standards.

In today's world, the concept of a patent as a free-standing entity that exists all by itself is somewhat outdated. It may be true to some degree in some industries, such as the chemical and pharmaceutical sectors, but it certainly is not the case in the computer, telecommunications and consumer electronics industries. You should therefore pay attention to the coexistence of many competing and complementary patents, because a multitude of other patents may overlap with the manufacture, sale or use of systems, products and services in your business.

# Starting with an invention

To be able to file a patent application one needs an invention and inventions can be created in any phase or part of business. Usually, but not necessarily always, inventions are produced during research and development activity. Inventions can be created internally within a company or arise from cooperation between companies or universities. They can also be bought from outside the company. Every invention requires the realisation of an inventive aspect and this is the element that one is attempting to protect when a patent application is filed. Sometimes it is present even though the inventor does not realise it or appreciate that his or her work product is an invention that could be patented.

In order to be patentable the invention must be: i) new or novel; ii) involve an inventive step; and iii) be industrially applicable (Figure 3.1). I explain these three requirements in more detail in the following sections.

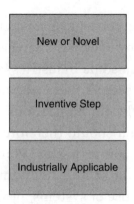

**Figure 3.1**  The three requirements for an invention to be patentable.

# New or novel

To qualify as new or novel, the invention must never have been made public anywhere in the world. In addition, it must be demonstrably different from publicly available ideas, inventions or products (so-called 'prior art'). This does not mean that every aspect of an invention must be novel. For example, new uses of known processes, machines, compositions of matter and materials are patentable and incremental improvements on known processes may also be patentable.

To determine whether an invention is new, one must look at the so-called 'state of the art' in play at the time of the first patent application. This includes the use of the product, all written and oral material available to the public and patent applications filed at the national patent office that are subsequently published. Providing that the invention does not fall within the state of the art at the time of application, it will be considered new.

Once an invention has been disclosed to the public, it cannot be patented. Such disclosure may occur through the publication of the invention, for example in a newspaper or magazine. However, this disclosure must include underlying principles of the invention, so much so that a competent reader would be able to reproduce the invention.

The legal definition and application of the novelty requirement differs between jurisdictions; where the requirement is stricter, the number of successful patent applications will subsequently be lower. The US is one of the more flexible jurisdictions; for example, disclosure abroad still permits an invention to be novel provided that it is not in written form.

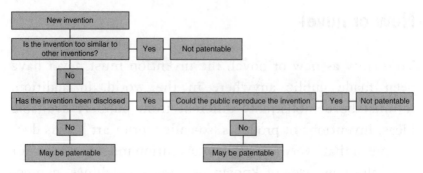

**Figure 3.2** Flowchart showing the novelty requirements for patent applications.

Figure 3.2 summarises these requirements for patent application.

## Inventive step

Whereas the novelty requirement tests whether the invention is actually known, the inventive step determines whether the invention would be obvious to a reasonably skilled worker. If, when the invention is compared with what is already known, it is not obvious to someone with good knowledge and experience of the subject, then it can be seen as an inventive step.

UK case law suggests that for the invention to be obvious, factors such as the nature of the problem solved by the invention, the significance of the problem, the duration of the problem and the demand for a solution, should all be considered (Haberman & Another *versus* Jackel International Ltd [1999]). The clearest modern test for determining the existence of an inventive step in the UK can be found in the

judgment in Molnycke AB *versus* Procter and Gamble Ltd
(1992). It asks the following questions:

- What is the inventive step?

- What was the state of the art at the priority date?

- In what respect does the step go beyond or differ from the
  state of the art?

- Would the step be obvious to a skilled person?

> *"An invention involves an inventive step if it is not*
> *obvious to a person skilled in the art."*   Section 3,
> The Patent Act 1977

In the US an invention is not patentable if its technical teaching would or could have been discovered by a person with
average skills in the respective field. Courts apply the 'non-
obviousness standard' (the US equivalent to inventive step)
and undertake a three-step factual inquiry that examines the
following:

... the scope and content of the prior art to which the invention pertains, the differences between the prior art and the
claims at issue, plus the level of ordinary skill in the relevant
art.

Courts then decide whether a person of ordinary skill could
reconcile the differences between the prior art and the claims
at issue, given the relevant prior art. An invention can
only be rendered obvious in the US where the prior art

specifically suggests that it would be obvious, unlike other jurisdictions where an implied judgment suffices. Consequently, just because an invention may have been predictable does not prevent its ability to be patented. Although such an approach may not be adopted elsewhere, it is generally accepted that one cannot rely on the luxury of hindsight when assessing an inventive step.

The reasonably skilled worker is presumed to possess the knowledge of the art at the date of the invention and to be familiar with all the relevant literature in that particular field of expertise. Where skilled individuals fail to produce an answer to the problem solved by the invention, it will prove difficult to suggest that the invention is obvious. It is general practice for the court to rely upon the evidence of experts in order to determine whether an inventive step exists.

The inventive step is often evaluated by considering the unexpected or surprising effect of the claimed invention. American courts, however, currently reject this approach and stress that patentable inventions may result from meticulous research, slow trial and error, or quite simply by luck.

The way the inventive step is interpreted will play an important role in determining whether an invention is patentable. The European Patent Office identifies the invention through adoption of the problem and solution approach and consequently the invention is seen as the solution to the specified problem in the patent application. However, this may not always be the most objective of sources and in such a case, the EPO has the ability to reformulate the problem by assessing the differences between the closest prior art and the invention. Courts in the UK have so far remained reluctant to apply the problem and solution approach and there has been little debate as to an alternative. Instead, courts assess the specification of an invention from the perspective of a person skilled in the relevant art.

## Industrially applicable

To be deemed industrially applicable, the invention must be capable of being used in some form of industry. In addition, the invention must have the ability to be reproduced or used in any kind of industry for it to be industrially applicable. This is consistent with the general approach, that a patent protects a technical solution to a problem, not simply an idea.

Courts tend to expect an invention to have a useful purpose, but what is considered 'useful' can differ, particularly in relation to patent law. An invention must be 'useful', inasmuch as it must be feasible; however, there is no need for it to be marketable for patent status to apply. The inventor must describe one effective way of carrying the invention into effect in its specification for the invention to be considered 'useful', and the test is therefore whether the invention will successfully carry out what is set out in the specification.

Countries differ in their treatment of industrial applicability and under US law certain developments that do not lead to an industrial product may be patented. An invention needs only to be operable and capable of satisfying some function or benefit to humanity. In other words, it must be useful! This usefulness concept is broader than the 'industrial applicability' concept required in Europe and other countries. The US rules permit the patentability of purely experimental inventions that cannot be made or used in an industry, or that do not feature a technical effect, as illustrated by the large number of patents granted in the US on 'methods of doing business'.

# Some facts and figures

## Overall volumes

The WIPO Patent Report, 2007 edition (available at http://www.wipo.int/ipstats/en/statistics/patents/patent_report_2007.html, and from where the quotes below are taken), gives some interesting facts, figures and trends to study, containing as it does information on volumes, growth areas and use of the PCT system. The report shows that worldwide filings of patent applications have grown at an average annual rate of 4.7%, with the highest growth rates experienced in North East Asian countries, particularly the Republic of Korea and China. The report is based on 2005 figures and shows that patents granted worldwide have increased at an average annual rate of 3.6% with some 600 000 patents granted in 2005 alone. By the end of 2005, approximately 5.6 million patents were in force worldwide.

The largest recipients of patent filings are the patent offices of Japan, the USA, China, the Republic of Korea and the European Patent Office (EPO). These five offices accounted for 77% of all patents filed in 2005 (a 2% increase over 2004) and represent 74% of all patents granted. With an increase of almost 33 % over 2004, the patent office of China became the third highest recipient of patent filings in 2005.

Use of the international patent system has increased markedly in recent years and although it remains highly concentrated, with 49 % of the estimated 5.6 million patents in force being owned by applicants from Japan and the USA, there is evidence of increasing use of the system by newly industrialising nations.

'We have witnessed a significant increase in the use of the patent system internationally in recent years,' said Dr. Kamil Idris, WIPO Director General. 'This is clearly one indicator of the level of inventiveness and innovation that is occurring around the world and signals those areas in which technological development is most pronounced.' He added, 'While the use of the system remains highly concentrated, we are seeing an historic evolution in the geography of innovation. With increased patenting activity in newly industrialising and emerging countries, we expect the pattern of ownership of patent rights worldwide will become more diversified over the coming years.'

Dr Idris also said, 'Information contained in patents and better analysis of data relating to patents is extremely valuable and for these reasons WIPO has enhanced its work relating to patent statistics. The current report is the most comprehensive yet, including an analysis of patenting activity by field of technology as well as improved statistical data on patent processing and patent life cycles.' He emphasised that this statistical data is useful and relevant to policy

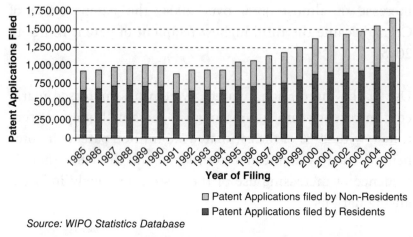

*Source: WIPO Statistics Database*

**Figure 3.3**    Patent applications filed by residents and non-residents.

makers, scientists, researchers and the business community (Figure 3.3).

## North East Asia: significant growth

The WIPO patent report reaffirms that North East Asia has significantly increased its share of worldwide patenting, both as a source of patent applications and as a target of non-resident patent applications from outside the region. Patent filings by residents doubled in the Republic of Korea and increased by more than eight fold in China between 1995 and 2005. The patent office of China has the highest growth rate for resident (+42.1 %) and non-resident (+23.6 %) filings.

Commenting on this significant shift in the geography of innovation, which for the past 250 years has been largely

focused in industrialised countries, Mr Francis Gurry, WIPO
Deputy Director General, who oversees WIPO's work relating to patents, predicted that this trend will continue. Based
on this report's findings (Figure 3.2), as well as trends in the
Patent Cooperation Treaty (PCT), Mr Gurry said 'Countries in
North East Asia will most likely continue to challenge their
counterparts elsewhere. A few years ago, they took the patent
world by surprise, but it is now very much the expectation

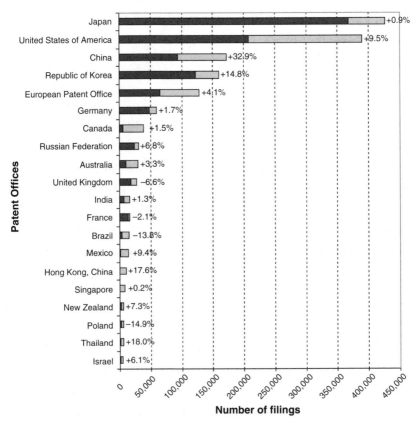

**Figure 3.4** Number of patent filings by country.

that countries like China and Korea will continue their rapid developments in innovation, one indicator of which is the number of patent applications filed.'

## The Patent Cooperation Treaty (PCT)

The WIPO patent report shows an increase in the use of the PCT, a multilateral pact administered by WIPO that provides a simplified system for international patent filing. International PCT applications increased by 7.9 % from 2005 to 2006 to reach 147 500, and at present 137 countries have signed up to the PCT.

Applicants from the USA are the largest filers of PCT international applications, followed by applicants from Japan and Germany. The number of PCT filings from North East Asian countries is increasing rapidly and filings in the Republic of Korea and China increased by 26.6 % and 56.5 %, respectively, from 2005 to 2006. Together, member states of the European Patent Convention account for 50 016 PCT international applications, representing an increase of 5.6 % from 2005.

> *"The PCT has now become the major route for international patent filing and WIPO is fully committed to further enhancing the system to ensure that it remains the efficient and cost-effective option for the international filing of patent applications."* Francis Gurry,
> WIPO Deputy Director General

# Patents granted in 2005

Some 600000 patents were granted in 2005 with the largest number of patents being granted by the patent office of the USA, followed by the offices of Japan, Korea (up two places from 2004), China (up one place from 2004) and the EPO. These five offices account for 74% of patents granted worldwide in 2005. Residents of Japan obtain the largest number of the patents granted worldwide, followed by residents of the USA, Korea, Germany and France.

Of the 5.6 million patents in force (the standard international rule provides that a patent may remain in force for up to 20 years), 90% are accounted for by ten offices: USA, Japan, Germany, Korea, United Kingdom, France, Spain, China, Canada and Russian Federation. Applicants from Japan and the USA owned 28% and 21%, respectively, of patents in force worldwide in 2005.

# Growth sectors

In its analysis of patent trends around the world, the WIPO patent report reveals an increase in filings in the electricity and electronics sectors (Figure 3.5). Patent applications filed in these areas represented 32% of worldwide patent filings between 2000 and 2004. Patent filings in this field of technology are concentrated in the patent offices of Japan and the USA, followed by Korea, the EPO and China. The three fastest growing technical fields from 2000 to 2004 were medical technology (+32.2%), audio-visual technology (+28.3%) and information technology (+27.7%).

| Technical Field | Year of Filing | | | | | Change compared with 2000 |
|---|---|---|---|---|---|---|
| | 2000 | 2001 | 2002 | 2003 | 2004* | |
| **I Electricity – Electronics** | | | | | | |
| 1 Electrical devices, electrical engineering, electrical energy | 113,432 | 117,374 | 112,553 | 113,902 | 127,969 | 12.8% |
| 2 Audio-visual technology | 87,479 | 94,220 | 89,349 | 94,986 | 112,197 | 28.3% |
| 3 Telecommunications | 102,720 | 112,365 | 104,513 | 106,696 | 115,494 | 12.4% |
| 4 Information technology | 110,701 | 125,036 | 115,272 | 118,572 | 141,357 | 27.7% |
| 5 Semiconductors | 64,049 | 71,367 | 68,082 | 67,271 | 78,483 | 22.5% |
| **II Instruments** | | | | | | |
| 6 Optics | 71,697 | 80,569 | 78,809 | 79,411 | 89,022 | 24.2% |
| 7 Analysis, measurement, control technology | 102,120 | 110,412 | 107,852 | 114,188 | 122,083 | 19.5% |
| 8 Medical technology | 55,813 | 59,415 | 61,569 | 72,229 | 73,789 | 32.2% |
| 9 Nuclear engineering | 5,920 | 5,922 | 5,820 | 6,029 | 6,752 | 14.1% |
| **III Chemistry – Pharmaceuticals** | | | | | | |
| 10 Organic fine chemistry | 36,625 | 36,137 | 37,447 | 37,574 | 34,790 | -5.0% |
| 11 Macromolecular chemistry, polymers | 46,698 | 46,728 | 43,918 | 44,073 | 42,244 | -9.5% |
| 12 Pharmaceuticals, cosmetics | 64,704 | 69,223 | 73,673 | 78,772 | 75,613 | 16.9% |
| 13 Biotechnology | 41,063 | 42,580 | 47,208 | 48,065 | 40,545 | -1.3% |
| 14 Agriculture and food | 19,857 | 20,822 | 22,873 | 24,187 | 22,237 | 12.0% |
| 15 Chemical and petrol industry, basic materials chemistry | 36,893 | 36,841 | 36,389 | 35,353 | 33,657 | -8.8% |
| 16 Surface technology, coating | 35,215 | 37,917 | 37,343 | 38,490 | 40,505 | 15.0% |
| 17 Materials, metallurgy | 38,087 | 39,985 | 36,625 | 37,100 | 35,891 | -5.8% |
| **IV Process engineering** | | | | | | |
| 18 Chemical engineering | 50,339 | 50,347 | 48,810 | 49,362 | 46,731 | -7.2% |
| 19 Materials processing, textiles, paper | 54,826 | 55,865 | 52,651 | 50,082 | 48,667 | -11.2% |
| 20 Handling, printing | 77,756 | 77,910 | 75,529 | 77,089 | 84,159 | 8.2% |
| 21 Agricultural and food processing, machinery and apparatus | 20,740 | 20,587 | 21,093 | 21,059 | 21,707 | 4.7% |
| 22 Environmental technology | 20,016 | 20,218 | 19,248 | 18,773 | 18,864 | -5.8% |
| **V Machinery – Mechanics – Transport** | | | | | | |
| 23 Machine tools | 38,454 | 39,563 | 35,664 | 34,834 | 36,435 | -5.2% |
| 24 Engines, pumps, turbines | 38,682 | 41,554 | 40,733 | 42,488 | 46,090 | 19.2% |
| 25 Thermal processes and apparatus | 27,005 | 27,382 | 26,196 | 26,066 | 26,943 | -0.2% |
| 26 Mechanical Components | 52,608 | 53,708 | 51,479 | 52,764 | 56,552 | 7.5% |
| 27 Transport | 68,833 | 70,112 | 67,185 | 72,146 | 79,781 | 15.9% |
| 28 Space technology and weapons | 5,418 | 5,414 | 5,370 | 5,811 | 5,351 | -1.2% |
| **VI Consumer goods – Civil engineering** | | | | | | |
| 29 Consumer goods and equipment | 84,889 | 87,505 | 85,395 | 88,112 | 95,193 | 12.1% |
| 30 Civil engineering, building, mining | 59,601 | 59,056 | 56,412 | 57,319 | 59,239 | -0.6% |

*Source: WIPO Statistics Database*
*adjusted data

**Figure 3.5**  Number of patent filings by technical field.

In 2006, 23% of published PCT international applications were classified in three technical fields, namely telecommunications, pharmaceuticals and cosmetics, and information technology. PCT international applications published in the field of semiconductors saw an increase of 28%, making this the fastest growing technical field in 2006, followed by information technology (+22%) and pharmaceuticals and cosmetics (+21%).

## Inventors

The WIPO patent report also examines the percentage and composition of foreign inventors in PCT international applications. It shows that companies of Switzerland, the Netherlands, Belgium and Sweden have an above average number of foreign inventors and researchers from Belgium, Austria, United Kingdom, Canada, Israel and India constituted the largest percentage of inventors working in foreign companies.

# Summary

The importance of patenting an invention is clear to see and failing to do so may prove catastrophic to a business. Patenting an invention is a decision that involves many factors, such as the cost and relative gains to be considered. As such, one should not patent every invention, as not only would this be a costly mistake, but it would also reduce the effectiveness of the patent system. Indeed, the requirements of novelty, inventive step and industrial applicability, act as a mechanism to preserve the quality of patents. In a factory, one commences with the raw materials needed to make the final product. Should the product be made with one of its components missing, the final product will not be the same as the others. It will be of a lower quality, it may not do what it was designed to do and as a result, if sold, it may result in customer dissatisfaction. All these factors apply to patent creation.

Many benefits arise from patenting an invention, and companies see high future value in patents and continue to invest in them. Today, it is more than just a few patent owners protecting inventions, because the IPR landscape is rapidly changing. Patents are big business and IPR strategy is becoming central for business strategy and the determining factor for the success of the company.

# 4

# Invention harvesting

## Introduction

In Chapter 2 you looked at the necessary elements in building
an overall Patent Creation Factory strategy, a strategy that
will act as a top-level action plan for your factory.

Innovation acts as the key raw material of your patent factory
and the quality of your ideas therefore have a direct outcome
on the success of what you set out to achieve. It is therefore
important to ensure not only that your ideas are of the highest
quality but also, if you wish to create a patent portfolio, that
there is a steady supply of those ideas.

This chapter aims to explain innovation and creativity,
because it is of critical importance that the factory really
appreciates this subject matter, and plays an active part creating and maintaining a culture of inventiveness within your
company.

Inventiveness is a subset of innovation. There are many innovative ideas that are not patentable, often based on the unique legal requirements outlined in the previous chapter. Fostering a culture of innovation and creativity within your company or organisation is not as such the sole responsibility of the Patent Creation Factory, but it certainly has a fundamental part to play. You need to appreciate that without such a culture being in place, you are unlikely to succeed.

## What is innovation?

Innovation can take many forms: it can be disruptive, transformative, radical, breakthrough or incremental in nature. It is most important to recognise and appreciate all these different forms as often the incremental form gets over-looked. Innovation literature typically distinguishes several separate stages of innovation. Generating or creating the idea is often seen as the first stage, but it is not the only one. Discussing the initial idea with others is a significant next step. Growing and developing the idea and adapting and modifying it as necessary is also a critical stage. Converting the specific innovative idea into something more concrete, whether that is a simulation model, a working prototype, a beta version, a formal proposal, etc. is also important. The initial stage often steals the limelight, but the other stages outlined are equally deserving of attention.

> *"When all think alike, then no one is thinking."*
> Walter Lippman

The process itself involves ambiguity, controversy and non-linearity. Innovation can take place in what is offered, who the defined customer is, and in how or where things are done. It may impact the product, the service, the process or the business model.

Creativity and innovation are key elements to survival and profitability in any business environment. Markets demand new products with better designs and more features at a lower price. Consequently, the effective management of innovation is a vital component of any successful business.

> *"Capital isn't so important in business. Experience isn't so important. You can get both these things. What is important is ideas. If you have ideas, you have the main asset you need, and there isn't any limit to what you can do with your business and your life."*
> Harvey Firestone

Innovation may be creating a new market that is in the presumed interests of the customer or changing the current provision of a product to better satisfy expressed customer needs. It may be simply improving a product currently on the market and enhancing its overall value to the customer, based on expressed feedback.

The significance of innovation cannot be underestimated. In fact, in a recent survey innovation was rated above cost cutting and mergers and acquisitions as a means to increase profitability and growth.

# A culture of innovation

Innovation starts with thinking differently. It is a process of questioning, experimenting, learning and adapting. It requires an appetite for risk, a willingness to question, an open mind to look at things without a predetermined conception, and perhaps most importantly, patience and perseverance.

Often, great innovation is done without any official sanctioning or target setting, just by individuals who found the time and the means to pursue their ideas. A permissive and supporting workplace fosters this kind of behaviour. The first step in creating an innovative culture is ensuring that your employees work in an atmosphere that permits them to have the necessary freedom to stray from what may be normal or ordinary in everyday work. They must be comfortable in their surroundings and have good relations with their fellow workers. Sufficient resources must be available to help them put some of these ideas into action. They should not be afraid to ask questions, because the answers, or lack thereof, may provide grounds for such innovation.

> *"Hire good people and leave them alone."*
> William McKnight

The nature of the systems, solutions, products and services that your company designs, manufacturers, distributes, sells and uses will have a direct bearing on the level of creativity within your company. As such, ask yourself, what types apply to your situation? Do you want to keep to these areas or do you want to enter new markets?

What time scales have you placed on your workers to improve your products and services? Too restrictive a time scale may not allow sufficient freedom for your workers to innovate, whereas one that is too relaxed may provide too much, resulting in an almost lazy attitude among your workers. Therefore, finding a balance is the key.

What types of research and development are taking place? These will have a direct impact on how you intend to improve a product, i.e., its design, its capabilities, etc.

Who are your contacts? Certain contacts specialise in different areas and, subsequently, who you have in your network has a direct bearing on the information you receive.

How qualified are your employees? To ask questions about the product and/or service your workers must understand it, which means that they may require a certain background or a certain qualification. There is no point having workers who don't understand the product or service you are providing because they will not raise the necessary questions or go through the thought processes required to come up with the solutions.

How does your company operate? What kind of support is in place and are there support structures to help new ideas take root? Are there rewards to encourage innovation? A strategic roadmap is an effective way to map out a series of major initiatives in an attack plan. A roadmap is simply a management group's view of how to get where they want to go or to achieve their desired objective.

One of the ways in which companies have tried to encourage innovation is by opening their research and development. Through collaborating with suppliers and customers, sharing software codes with programmers and tapping networks of scientists and entrepreneurs, they aim to broaden their level of feedback while gaining a greater understanding of the demand and response to their products and services. This is called 'open innovation'.

Senior management plays a lead role in promoting innovation within the most innovative businesses, creating a positive climate and culture for innovation and entrepreneurship. For example, they foster creativity and innovation by allowing time off for scouting; they are not overly risk averse and invest in the occasional high-risk project; and they encourage projects and teams working outside the business. Senior management also nurtures a team culture, fosters effective cross-functional new product development teams, and provides strong support and empowerment to these teams.

Part of creativity resides in the fact that you are delving into the unknown, and because predicting the result of an uncertainty is impossible, this may be too great a risk for many people. Balancing this risk, however, is that you simply cannot afford to be too pessimistic in your approach. Innovation is not just something that appears. Building a creative company takes synchronisation from the centre, cross boundary collaboration and structural changes to the organisational chart.

Customer insight is also essential. The most innovative companies build in a strong customer focus into their systems and rely heavily on customer-based research in the early days of projects. They often invest heavily by doing their home-work before development resulting in the creation of differen-tiated superior customer-built products to their competitors. This is where they gain their competitive advantage.

Boston Consulting Group (BCG) recently released their 'Inno-vation 2006' study report. Their report indicated that innova-tion remains a top-level strategic focus for many companies, with the majority of executives who were surveyed ranking it a top-three strategic priority. The report highlighted that innovation does translate into superior long-term perform-ance and furthermore, innovators have helped to increase profit margins and maintain revenue growth. There were a number of interesting results and insights in this study, in particular concerning the attributes of an innovative company. BCG asked the executives why they thought their company was innovative and then summarised the results for the top five. The following attributes were highlighted: an innovative culture, a deep customer understanding, and market focus.

> *"Companies have to nurture [creativity and motivation] – and have to do it by building a compassionate yet performance-driven corporate culture. In the knowledge economy the traditional soft people side of our business has become the new hard side."* Gay Mitchell – Executive VP, HR, Royal Bank

# Harvesting inventions

Several key elements need to be incorporated when planning a strategy for the successful production of inventions, including a focused portfolio management, an effective and flexible 'idea to patent' process, a culture of innovation and a well developed process for defining and agreeing new filing targets (Figure 4.1).

However, although these are all important elements, it is important to note that there is no single avenue to success and focusing your strategy around any one of these elements does not guarantee success. All these elements are commonly seen in the most innovative of companies and are now being used by businesses wishing to emulate their competitors' success.

Senior management and a strategic vision of the business usually drive successful invention harvesting. A strategy provides direction and helps to steer the allocation of resources as well as aid with the selection of certain projects over others. A successful Patent Creation Factory strategy should

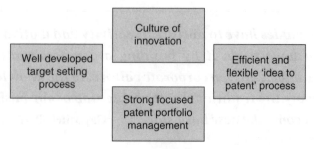

**Figure 4.1**   Elements needed for the successful production of inventions.

incorporate clearly defined invention targets and clearly defined roles for each invention. There should also be specified areas of strategic focus and a willingness to commit in the long term.

It is important that a company identifies and communicates to its employees how each invention will fit in with the overarching business strategy. This may involve specifying the collective goals of the business and indicating the rôle that each invention will play in helping it to achieve these goals. It is vital that this aspect is accurately and clearly communicated throughout the business in order to ensure that everyone involved is working towards a common purpose.

## Summary

Ideas are the raw material of your patent factory and their quality will have a direct bearing on the success of your aims. Therefore, you need to ensure that your ideas are of the highest quality and that you have a steady supply of them. You should appreciate that not all ideas are patentable, and even if they are patentable, you may not want to do so.

Your key supplier of these ideas is the responsible inventor community. This critical group will be discussed in detail in Chapter 6.

You need to play an active part in fostering a culture of innovation. You need to fully understand the business drivers for innovation and the demand for innovative products and services. You also need to be at ease dealing with the inventor community and their issues and concerns. Being able to spot innovative people or behaviour as well as being able to recognise the different ways that people absorb and process information and create ideas are key aspects of your role. You must endeavour to support not stifle creative approaches, and identify barriers to innovation where they exist. You must recognise the different ways that people communicate information and ideas, and learn how to manage the level of detail in such communication effectively. Communication between the Patent Creation Factory and the inventor community is all-important. Among the key skills and competencies you need are the ability to: use language to support and encourage the discussion and implementation of innovative ideas; use techniques to challenge ideas constructively; and use constructive feedback to build confidence, and motivate and foster innovation. You must also be able to define approaches to help manage innovative teams and creative individuals, because it is most likely that you will be involved in such activities. You must be willing through words and actions to support open discussion of new ideas and you must understand some of the key factors in motivating people and creating an innovative culture.

# 5

# Core activities of
# patent creation

IN CHAPTER 3 YOU EXAMINED WHY YOU MAY WANT TO
patent your invention and in this chapter I look at
how you would go about doing it. This is the part
of the patenting process where you get to see your
patent coming together. In the factory analogy, it is the
equivalent of starting out with the raw materials and step-
by-step watching a different part of the product being
assembled. At the end of this process you will have your
fully assembled product, that is, you will have your
patent.

The core activities of patent creation are effectively the same
no matter which process you choose. However, there are
certain advantages to each procedure depending upon the
nature of your invention and the scope of the protection you
seek. Small differences also exist in what each route may
require of you and it is therefore useful to consider each core
activity individually.

There are three routes to choose. First, you may decide that you only want to protect your invention in your own country or maybe a few others, in which case the simplest route is just to apply to the national offices of the countries in which you seek protection. However, it is important to realise that each country has its own rules and procedural requirements will certainly differ. As such I have chosen the UK application procedure as an example of a national route, but have compared it with the USA to highlight key differences between the two systems. Second, if you decide that you wish to extend your protection to a geographic area, spanning more than several countries, the regional route will prove most suitable. In this regard I look at the European Patent Convention (EPC). Finally, should you desire to have protection of a more international scope, the Patent Cooperation Treaty (PCT) would be more suitable.

# A national application – the UK

For a typical patent application in the UK, it takes between two and three years before a patent is granted, although the UK Patent Office can accelerate this procedure if you make your need for haste known. In essence there are five stages before you are granted a patent: completing the application; filing it with the appropriate patent office; requesting an initial examination and search of the prior art; publication of your application; and requesting a more substantial examination (Figure 5.1).

An application for a patent should include a full description of your invention, a set of claims defining your

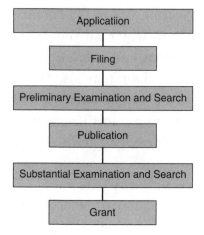

**Figure 5.1**  The stages of obtaining a patent.

invention, a short abstract summarising the technical features of your invention and a completed application form. Drafting an application is a difficult task because patent applications are technical, commercial and legal documents. Therefore, they are written with a number of different purposes in mind and to avoid duplicating the prior art you should try to make the claims as narrow as possible. However, in order to achieve the maximum protection from the patent, the claims must be drafted as widely as possible. A balance must be sought and it is advisable that you leave this to your patent agent. The general rule is that applicants are required to disclose only such details of the invention as to enable a person skilled in the art to reproduce it. This means that a patent does not need to reveal important features about the invention, such as the cheapest or strongest materials to use or even the best way in which to use the invention.

In the UK you are encouraged to file your patent as early as possible. Provisions are made to allow this without the complete satisfaction of the initial requirements necessary to be granted a patent. Section five of the Patent Act 1977 grants a period of 12 months in which all you need to submit at first is a request for a patent and a description of the invention, although sometimes a claim may also be required. This grace period allows you time to consider which markets to enter, whether you should perform further experiments and whether to seek investors. Where you have several rivals pursuing the same or similar lines of research as yourself, it is vital for you to establish a priority date ahead of your competitors because any infringements will be backdated from this date. This is also the date on which the state of the art will be assessed in order to judge the novelty of your invention and it is therefore crucial that this date is as early as possible so that the comparable level of the state of the art is restricted. Furthermore, the UK is party to the Paris Convention and subsequently you will have a 12 month period to file an application in any other member state that is party to the Convention. It is important to realise that it is not always beneficial to file an application too early, because initially you may not recognise the full technical or commercial capability of your invention. As a result your claim may be too narrow, allowing competitors to 'invent round' the patent. Moreover, it may be discovered during examination by the patent office or during revocation proceedings, that the invention does not satisfy the requirements of patentability. It is therefore essential that the application be filed neither too early nor too late. As in many situations, timing is everything. After this 12 month period, should a full application not be submitted, the application will be assumed to have lapsed.

Within a year from the filing date an initial examination and search must be sought. In this examination, the examiner determines whether your application complies with the formal requirements, namely, that it contains a request for a grant, a description of your invention, one or more claims and an abstract. The examiner also ensures that the inventor has been identified and that other formalities, such as payment of fees, have been satisfied. Once the examiner is satisfied, you receive a report that states the conclusions and gives you a chance to make amendments. The aim of the search is to identify documents that may prove useful during the later substantive examination. These documents show the state of the relevant prior art and this is summarised in another report.

To guarantee that the requirement of 'unity of invention' is met, the application is also examined to ensure that it only relates to one invention or a group of inventions that share a 'single inventive concept'. Where it is found that two or more inventions are claimed in a single application, this require-ment will not be satisfied unless it is decided that they have a single inventive concept. For this to occur, the inventions must possess the same 'special technical features', features that define the contribution that each invention makes to the prior art. Should the application cover more than one invention, the search will be limited to the initial invention defined in the claims. The applicant may then decide to split the initial application so that each invention discovered may be submitted individually. This is permitted provided that the appropriate fees are paid and no new material is added to the initial application. The priority date of the initial application will also be extended to include these further applications.

The UK Patent Office's web site (http://www.ipo.gov.uk/ patent/p-applying/p-costtime.htm) provides a tool that you can use to perform an initial search for prior art before completing your application and in order to ensure that your invention is indeed novel. This can prove particularly useful because it may save you both time and money. The European Patent Office (EPO) has developed a free patent search service called 'esp@cenet', which contains access to the databases of over 20 European national patent offices, the database of the EPO itself and that of the World Intellectual Property Office (WIPO). Although this tool should not be relied upon to provide conclusive results as to the patentability of your invention, it does help to determine its novelty. Apart from 'esp@cenet' the EPO also provides numerous other tools that can be used to search for prior art. Despite being useful, it is advisable that alongside these tools you also hire a patent attorney or request the patent office to perform an expert search of all prior art.

The UK Patent Office also offers a patentability search, which further to testing the novelty of your invention also measure its inventiveness. The results will subsequently enable you to produce a more accurate scope when drafting your patent claims and this again can save you both time and money. You will be sent a report that lists all the areas searched, highlighting all relevant prior art, and you may then discuss this with the searcher at any time. This service provides invaluable feedback that aids you if you need to redraft your claims. Costs for patentability searches vary depending on their technical difficulty.

You are obliged to publish your application within 18 months of your filing date to allow for public inspection. The purpose behind such a rule is to allow third parties the opportunity to make observations as to whether they believe a patent should be granted, and also allows any other patent seekers to observe how an examiner may react to a similar application, should they be considering such a possibility. Publication of the application also ensures that third parties can discover whether they are infringing the rights of another.

There are both advantages and disadvantages associated with the requirement of publication and inevitably, by publishing the details of your invention, rivals will use this information to develop your invention further or 'invent around' it. However, on the positive side, publication signifies that you have won the so-called 'patent race', and if the patent is subsequently granted, you may claim damages for infringement from the date of publication.

Following publication of your application it must be examined one more time. This examination goes into the mechanics of the application, rather than the general formalities that the previous examination considered, and your application is examined to ensure that it fulfils the requirements of patentability and is compatible with the Patents Act 1977. The invention must satisfy the requirements of novelty, industrial applicability and involve an inventive step. Furthermore, your application must be sufficiently disclosed and the claims must be concise and supported by the accompanying description. This examination must occur within six months of publication and within four and a half years of the initial application, in which time the examiner will submit a report raising any objections as to the patentability of the invention. Once again, you are given the opportunity to persuade the examiner otherwise or amend your application. Should you fail to come to an agreement with the examiner it is possible to raise the issue in a formal hearing before a senior examiner, with the further possibility of appeal. Although this route is available, formal proceedings are very rare within the UK system.

Assuming that all the requirements are satisfied, you will be informed of your successful application and a certificate issued to you confirming the grant of the patent and the publication of the decision. The patent initially provides you with an exclusive proprietary right of four years. Upon entering the fifth year renewal fees are required annually and failure to pay these results in the lapse of your patent. It is important to be vigilant because this period will come much sooner than expected. The 20 year period is calculated from the date on which your application was first filed and this will generally be anything up to four and a half years earlier. As a result, renewal fees may be due within six months of the patent being granted. The patent takes effect once it has been published in the Official Journal.

# Key differences between the UK and US systems

In the previous section we looked at the steps that are involved and the relevant legal requirements in an application for a patent in the UK. But the UK is just one example of a national application procedure and it is important to compare it with another jurisdiction in order to highlight that although an abundance of similarities exist between most countries' application procedures, you must be aware that being successful in an application in one country does not guarantee you the same result in another. Indeed alongside different procedural requirements, attitudes also differ and will have an effect on the general willingness of a patent office to grant your desired patent. I have opted to use the American system as a comparison to the application procedure set out above. The following differences are by no means a comprehensive list of all the inconsistencies between the two procedures, but the aim is to pick out several key examples that symbolise how requirements and procedural elements may differ.

Perhaps most importantly, the majority of countries tend to follow the 'first to file' rule in which the first person to file the invention gains the right to apply for a patent. The USA, on the other hand, has adopted an alternative approach whereby the first person to invent a product or process gains this right. In the US, the inventor is always the applicant whereas in the UK, and in fact the rest of Europe, the applicant can be a legal entity other than the inventor, for example an employer. In addition, the US has a grace period, which allows inventors to disclose their inventions before applying for a patent, but similar action in the UK will invalidate any subsequent application. The US Patent and Trademark Office also requires that the best mode of performing the invention is described in the specification. In the UK there is no such requirement; although you must include a way to perform/use your invention, it does not necessarily have to be the best way. In the US, a patent can be obtained where additional material has been added at a later date to an existing disclosure from a pending application and this creates a so-called Continuation-in-Part or CIP application. The UK is consistent in its approach with the rest of Europe, in that two separate applications would be required in such a scenario and each would be subject to the usual patentability requirements. In Europe it is standard to use two-part claims. Such claims are known as Jepson claims in the US and are not the preferred method. Finally, the US Patent and Trademark Office tends to look more favourably on granting patents to business methods and software.

# A regional application – the EPC

The European Patent Convention is an example of a regional application that is exclusive to Europe. Other regional patenting agreements exist, such as the Protocol on Patents and Industrial Designs within the framework of the African Regional Intellectual Property Organisation (ARIPO), also known as the ARIPO Harare Protocol, and the Eurasian Patent Convention. The EPC created a single procedure for the grant of patents within Europe, the result of which is an easier, cheaper and ultimately better form of protection for inventions in the contracting states of the Convention. This route should definitely be considered if you seek protection in several of the contracting states, because it proves more beneficial than taking out individual protection in each of the national offices. The European patent gives you the equivalent rights but at a fraction of the time, effort and cost. European patents may also be effective in countries that have not yet acceded to the EPC but which have agreed cooperation and European extension agreements. At present this includes Albania, Croatia, Latvia, Lithuania and the Former Yugoslavian Republic of Macedonia. It is important to distinguish between the direct European route (the EPC) and the Euro-PCT route (see below).

The European grant procedure starts with a formalities examination and a compulsory search, which is then followed by publication of the application and the search report. After this a more substantive examination takes place before the patent is granted. This may lead to opposition proceedings in certain cases.

Article 52(1) EPC states that European patents are granted for inventions that are new, involve an inventive step and are susceptible of industrial application. To this extent you may have noticed that these requirements are common to the UK and US patentability requirements already examined. On the whole you will notice that the patentability requirements tend not to differ significantly between countries, however it is often the rigidity with which each national patent office applies these requirements that distinguishes between them.

An invention is considered to be new, within the meaning of the EPC, if it does not form part of the state of the art. Article 54(2) EPC provides a definition of the state of the art as 'comprising everything made available to the public anywhere in the world by means of a written or oral description, by use, or in any other way, before the date of filing or priority'. It sets a very wide definition in order to limit the scope of what is to be considered 'novel'.

The EPO carries out a search of all prior art and issues you with a search report. You can also request, free of charge, an Extended European Search Report, which acts as a non-binding opinion on the patentability of your application. This report provides invaluable feedback, because not only does it allow you to amend your application but also, if your application is deemed to have no chance of success, you can withdraw the application and save any potential costs you may have later incurred.

Your European patent application must disclose your invention in a manner that is sufficiently clear and complete for it to be carried out by a person skilled in the art. It must relate to a single invention only or to a group of inventions that can be linked to form a single concept.

When drafting your description you must specify the technical field to which your invention relates, indicate any background art of which you are aware, and disclose the invention as claimed. Your description must also briefly describe what is shown in any drawings, describe at least one way your invention may be used and indicate how it is 'susceptible of industrial application'.

The claims must define the invention and its scope will have a direct bearing on the level of protection granted. They must be clear, concise and supported by the description and they should really be in two parts, prior art and characterising parts, although this is not essential. The prior art section should designate the subject matter of the invention and the technical features needed to define it. The characterising part should state the technical features for which protection is sought. The application cannot contain more than one independent claim, although it may be followed by one or more 'dependant' claims. Article 84 EPC requires the claims to be 'no more than necessary' and 'reasonable'. The wording you use in your claims must leave no doubt as to their meaning and scope and should be consistent with the description. The area defined by the claims must be as precise as possible and should not define the invention in terms of the result it intends to achieve. If your application contains more than 10 claims at the time of filing you must pay a claims fee for each claim over the 10th claim. These fees must be paid within one month of filing the application and failure to pay results in these additional claims being abandoned.

The abstract must contain a precise summary of the disclosure contained in the description, claims and drawings and should highlight the relevant technical field, while also giving a clear account of the problem, its solution and how the invention should be used.

Your application must not contain statements or drawings that are contrary to public order or morality. Nor should it contain statements disparaging the inventions of any third party or the merits or validity of their applications or patents. Mere comparisons though are permitted.

Once you have filed your application you are unable to make any amendments to the description, the claims or any drawings that extend beyond the applications content. As such you cannot add examples or features to the application to remedy any deficiencies you discover at a later date in the disclosure. You are also prohibited from extending the subject matter of the claims unless there is clear support for it. Therefore, it is imperative that you ensure the claims are filed both clearly and accurately and that they identify the invention that you wish to protect.

You can file European patent applications at the EPO in Munich, its branch in The Hague, or its sub-office in Berlin, or at the central industrial property office or any other competent authority of a contracting state if the law of that state so permits. The date of filing accorded to applications filed directly at the EPO is the date on which they are handed in or posted. The date of filing accorded to applications filed electronically is the date on which the application documents are received at the EPO or the competent national authority.

In respect of a European patent application you are required to pay a filing fee, a search fee, a claims fee where appropriate, designation fees and extension fees where appropriate. You must pay the filing and search fees (and any claims fees) within one month of filing and the designation and any extension fees must be paid within six months of the date on which the European Patent Bulletin mentions publication of the European search report. If you fail to pay the filing, search or designation fees in due time your application is deemed to have been withdrawn.

Your application will be published 18 months after your filing or priority date. Should you be in a rush you can request for it to be published even earlier and your description, claims, drawings, abstract and search report will all be published for public inspection. The EPO informs you of the exact date on which your search report will be mentioned in the European

Patent Bulletin and you will be reminded of the time period in which you are required to request an examination. Furthermore, from this point you have six months in which you must pay your designation fees.

The substantive examination must be requested, in writing, within six months of the European Patent Bulletin mentioning your search report. Three technically qualified examiners carry this examination out, on occasions joined by a legally qualified examiner, although generally the examination is entrusted to just one of the technically qualified examiners. In the case of oral proceedings, however, these will be held before the full examining division. In either case, the full division makes the final decision on the grant of the patent.

The examiners examine whether your application and invention meet the requirements of the Convention and whether it is patentable. Before their first communication to you, you are entitled to file 'substantive observations' on the search report and amend the description, claims and drawings. If the examiner responsible objects for any reasons he or she informs you, inviting your comments and resulting amendments. At this point you can amend your application by filing replacement pages, annotating a copy of the relevant pages or indicating any changes made in a letter. If you still cannot come to an agreement at this stage, the examiner continues with the examination and issues either a further written communication to you informing you of the objections or contacts you in person or by telephone. If at any stage you are unhappy with the examiner's objections, you may request oral proceedings.

If the examining division is of the opinion that a European patent cannot be granted, your application is rejected. The division as a whole takes this decision, not just the individual examiner, and the reasons for the rejection are communicated to you. On the other hand, if your application and invention meet the requirements of the Convention, the examining division will grant a European patent on condition that all the fees have been paid and the claims have been translated into the other two official languages of the EPO, other than the language you initially chose.

The grant does not take effect until the date it is mentioned in the European Patent Bulletin. At the same time, the patent office publishes a European patent specification, which contains your description, claims and drawings and certifies your patent.

To keep your patent alive you must pay renewal fees to the EPO and these become due after three years of protection and must then be paid annually. They fall on the last day of the month in which the anniversary of the date of filing falls. Payment may still be validly made up to six months after the due date, provided that an additional fee of 10% is paid within this period. If you fail to pay the renewal fee your application is deemed to have been withdrawn.

Should your application be rejected you may wish to appeal. Decisions on appeals are presided over by a board of appeal and you must provide notice of your appeal, which should be filed in writing within two months after the date you contested the decision to reject your application. Within four months you must file a written statement specifying the reasons for your appeal. This should give a succinct but full account of your arguments.

Opposition proceedings occur when a third party is not happy with the granting of your patent. This can occur anytime up to nine months of your patent being mentioned in the Patent Bulletin. The opposition division is set up similarly to the examining division, but instead of judging the patentability of your application, it examines the opposition brought. An opposition may only be filed on limited grounds, namely that the subject matter of your patent may not be patentable, that you have failed to clearly disclose your invention sufficiently for a skilled person to perform it or its subject matter extends beyond the content of your application. The EPO will notify you of the objection and determine whether it is admissible. Any deficiencies in the opposition are notified to the relevant party and they are given a period to amend their opposition accordingly.

# An 'international' application – the PCT

The Patent Cooperation Treaty (PCT) allows you to obtain protection for your invention in any or all of the contracting countries to the treaty. It is important to note that although it is often referred to as an 'international' application, there is in reality no application procedure that protects an invention in every country of the world; however, the PCT is the closest thing to one.

Similar to the EPC, you need to file only one patent application that has effect in several countries rather than have to go through the hassle and extra expenditure of applying to each national office. The PCT differs from the EPC, however, in that the EPC is an example of a regional application, limited to the European zone, whereas the PCT has contracting countries from all over the world. Therefore, if you are looking for an application more international in its nature, this is the best route for you. However, it is important to note that the prosecuting of the application still lies at the hands of each national authority.

The PCT procedure consists of two main phases: an 'international phase' and a 'national and/or regional phase'. The international phase covers the filing of the application and its processing, the establishment of the international search report and written opinion, the publication of the international application and search report, and optionally, an international preliminary examination and report on patentability. This report analyses the general patentability of your invention. Together with the published international application and international search report, the preliminary patentability report is communicated to the relevant national or regional offices and subsequently begins the 'national and/or regional phase' of the PCT procedure. This stage involves paying the required fees, providing any necessary translations and appointing a patent agent where required, all of which must be performed within the necessary time frame. Where any deadlines have not been met, the application is deemed to be suspended. Should you satisfactorily perform what is required of you, the next stage is for your application to be examined further for compatibility with local laws, before finally being refused or granted.

There are several clear advantages of the PCT application. First, it saves effort, time and workload because under the PCT you are required to file only one application, in one place, in one language and pay one set of initial fees. Second, the division between the two phases enables you to submit an international application and then have a significant time period to decide to which national/regional offices you wish to apply. This is helpful in that you can assess the development of the relevant market at this time and carry out further economic analysis in order to decide in which states you need to seek protection for your invention. In addition, there are a number of materials and mechanisms that, in the meantime, provide you with further information as to the likely outcome of your application. Subsequently, this gives you the chance to make any necessary amendments. Third, you are given a great deal of instruction and advice in the form of the international search report, written by a patent officer with a wealth of experience in examining patent applications. As such it provides a very accurate feedback mechanism and should you be told that your application is rejected for any one of a number of reasons, you save the expense that you would have incurred by continuing with the proceedings. Another form of feedback is the written opinion of the International Searching Authority, which gives an initial non-binding opinion on whether the claimed invention satisfies the formal requirements of novelty, inventive step and industrial applicability. Finally, if you request an international preliminary examination, you have the opportunity to enter into dialogue with the examiner of the International Preliminary Examining Authority and amend your application based on the conclusions of the examiner.

# Summary

You should have noticed by now that, in general, the overall procedure from application to grant tends not to differ too much between countries. No matter which route you select, you will be required to file an application, request an initial examination and search, satisfy the patentability requirements of novelty, inventive step and industrial applicability, have your application published and request another, more substantial, examination and search. After all of this, your application, no matter what your chosen route, will be protected for a 20 year period subject to the annual payments of renewal fees. The main differences tend to be the obvious scope of the protection granted, and inevitably dates and time limits tend to differ, as do the costs. The EPC and PCT require designation fees and the translation of your application, and one could make the argument that the EPC and PCT procedures provide greater feedback to the applicant throughout the procedure, which enables you to amend your application and subsequently improve your chance of success. With little to choose between the routes it is for you to decide which best suits your intentions. The key question is ultimately do you seek protection on a national, regional or international scale? Of course certain factors such as the resources at your disposal and the nature of your invention will play an instrumental part in shaping your answer.

I stated at the beginning of this chapter that the patenting process was the equivalent of starting out with raw materials in a factory and step-by-step assembling until you have your finished product. Even if you start off with the best raw materials, poor machinery can damage them to the extent that the product becomes low in quality. Through investing in your machinery and ensuring that everything is done properly the end product will reflect the quality of your raw materials. Similarly, allocating the necessary time and resources to your application will therefore ensure that your patent is of the highest quality.

# References

EPO web site: Guide for Applicants

PCT Applicant's Guide: International Phase, WIPO

# 6

# The inventor community

## Introduction

The Patent Creation Factory cannot exist in isolation. There are a number of critical interfaces to manage and relationships to develop and maintain, in order to ensure that the factory successfully creates the highest quality patents. Although this book is centred round the patent factory, this chapter looks *outside* the factory, examining the most critical group of relevance to the Patent Creation Factory, namely the inventor community.

## Categorising the inventor community

It is important to recognise that ideas may come from many sources. The inventor community is the collection of individuals who supply the innovation, creativity and ideas, which act as the basic raw materials in the Patent Creation Factory.

There is not, however, one homogenous community of inventors and it is worth sub-dividing this inventor community into several groups or categories and then rating them individually.

The sub-groups or categories may be defined as follows:

- 'serial' inventors (the people who come up with good ideas on a regular basis);

- inventors in your company who have submitted only one or two inventions in the past;

- employees who have never submitted an invention or an idea;

- employees who submit ideas to others interested in ideas and innovation within the company but not necessarily to the intellectual property rights (IPR) function;

- employees working on leading edge technology, products and services within your company;

- component suppliers, parts vendors, application developers and content providers, all outside your company but with links and relationships to it;

- partners with whom you may jointly design and develop products and/or services;

- customers who purchase your products and/or services;

- end-users of your products and/or services;

- unsolicited ideas received from the general public.

Obviously, some sub-groups are well defined whereas others are somewhat vague, and there may very well be an overlap between some of the segments or categories listed above. It is not a mistake that some of the sub-groups or categories listed have not historically submitted ideas to the Patent Creation Factory. Just because they have not done so in the past, does not mean that they may not unilaterally do so, or be approached to do so, in the future.

> *"If I have a thousand ideas and only one turns out to be good, I am satisfied."*     Alfred Bernhard Nobel

# Rating these inventor community sub-groups

I mentioned above about rating these sub-groups and although it may not be possible to do so in a formal manner, it is clear that you do need to distinguish between these sub-groups in terms of how you spend your Patent Creation Factory time and energy.

One way to rate each sub-group or category is as follows:

- skill and competency level;

- volume of ideas;

- quality of ideas;

- ease of linking and communicating with them;

- extent to which they 'push' their ideas to the Patent Creation Factory or the extent to which the factory 'pulls' the idea from the inventor;

- directness of ideas to the factory from the inventor, i.e., direct from inventor to the factory or via some other route.

Another way to consider rating the inventor is by matching the inventor to the form of innovation that is being submitted. As discussed in Chapter 4, innovation can take many forms. It can be disruptive, transformative or incremental in nature. Innovation can take place in what is being offered, to whom it is being offered, in how things are done or in where things are done. It may impact the product, the service, the process or the business model, so you may wish to consider incorporating the nature of the innovation when rating the inventor.

Just as any traditional factory needs to understand and appreciate the source, volume, quality and logistics of the raw materials and product components being supplied into their factory, the very same applies to our patent factory.

## Working with inventors inside the company or organisation

The term serial inventor refers to those who regularly submit good quality inventions to the Patent Creation Factory, such as your top inventors. They have a proven track record and are at ease working with the factory. This group is a critical group as far as the factory is concerned because they not only supply critical raw material to the factory but also may help to mentor and coach others to become serial inventors.

> *"Innovation is the whim of an elite before it becomes a need of the public."*   Ludwig von Mises

Some inventors may only submit one or two ideas, perhaps due to a lack of experience or maybe because their first ideas were met with a poor response from the Patent Creation Factory. It may be worth discussing with some such inventors about their general experiences interfacing to the factory. What worked well and what didn't work so well? How easy or difficult was it for the inventor to submit the idea, and what was the initial reaction and feedback to the inventor from the factory? How was the inventor informed about the decisions taken by the factory? Was there any coaching mechanism in place to provide assistance to the inventor to help him or her submit the idea? If the idea from the inventor was accepted and then progressed through the patenting process, how then did you keep the inventor informed of the progress of his or her idea? It is worth noting that many good ideas are not patentable, but just because it is not patentable does not necessarily mean that it is not a good idea. It is worth remembering this when rejecting an idea from an inventor.

How well are you linked to those other groups and functions within your company, which are involved in gathering ideas, or generally concerned with innovation and creativity? It is important to recognise that the Patent Creation Factory is unlikely to be the only function in a company looking for ideas and innovation. Are there other individuals, groups or functions within your company or organisation with a special interest in the subject of creativity and innovation? Are there people focused on new business opportunities, venturing or start-ups? Is there a quality group working on process and product improvements? The patent factory should be linking to such groups or individuals to foster cooperation. Those who are submitting ideas to such groups may not even consider themselves inventors, and so will surely be pleased to be approached.

# Working with inventors external to your company or organisation

In the past, most Patent Creation Factories have tended to focus on getting ideas and invention reports from the inventor community within the company and in particular from those with a track record of submitting ideas and inventions, our so-called 'serial' inventors. Most Patent Creation Factories have also tended to focus on those working in the research and development area of the company and have perhaps neglected those in other disciplines such as manufacturing, service and repair, logistics and distribution and marketing among others. Most patent factories have also tended to neglect inventors based outside the company or organisation. A few questions to ask follow below.

Do you have the processes and systems in place to handle ideas coming from sources other than your own employees?

Are you working with perhaps general legal, sourcing and/or purchasing, to ensure intellectual property terms and conditions are built into contracts with key suppliers and vendors? In those contracts, have you included information and guidance regarding the submission of ideas arising from that cooperation?

Do you have processes and systems to handle ideas sent directly to your Patent Creation Factory from the general public?

Have you considered actively acquiring ideas, patent applications or granted patents from external third parties?

Is your Patent Creation Factory working closely with University Relations and are you familiar with your own company's key university or college relationships? Are you aware of all key joint research projects planned or which are currently underway and how well do you understand and appreciate the patent policies or guidelines of these particular universities or colleges? Are there differences between their thinking and yours that have to be resolved?

How are you linked to individuals or groups in your company who have direct contact with your customers or end-users and thus have access to their comments, feedback and suggestions concerning your products and services? Do you have the balance right between encouraging the submission of ideas and 'protecting' yourself?

Dell Computer's 'Idea-Storm' is just one example of a method adopted by a company to enable the public to submit its ideas.

Any individual can go onto a site and post an idea. Other users will then choose to either promote or demote the idea. This forum allows Dell to pick up new ideas and also acts as a useful feedback tool to suggest whether the idea is a good one or not; it also helps gain a general understanding as to which improvements are desired from existing products and the response such changes receive from the public. Furthermore, the site also provides a forum allowing Dell employees to interact with the public and discuss ideas.

> *"We will acquire 50% of our invovations from outside P & G."*    A. G. Lafley, President and Chief Executive, The Procter & Gamble Company

Some ideas may come from external sources such as other companies, partners in joint development work, universities or the general public. What additional issues need to be taken into account when patenting ideas coming from these sources and how does a company make sure that it has the right to claim the idea as its own? It is sometimes difficult to share a patent between companies or between an individual and a company, so mechanisms need to be put in place to ensure that there is no dispute over the ownership of the patent and that both parties are treated fairly.

Just as a normal factory will ask questions of itself to gain a better understanding of its operations and raw materials, all these questions need to be answered in order to ensure the smooth running of your patent factory.

Dealing with an external inventor is always that bit more complex compared to dealing with an internal inventor. You would like to pay as little as possible for the other person's idea, plus obtain the best indemnification possible, full ownership of the patent and broad and free licences for any background related intellectual property. The external inventor would get nothing! However the real world does not work like that, and a win-win solution has to be found.

# Understanding inventors

It is important to step into the shoes of inventors and in particular understand how they work and think, plus how they may perceive the Patent Creation Factory and intellectual property in general.

Innovative people may be classified as shown in Figure 6.1.

| | | |
|---|---|---|
| Engineers | versus | Inventors |
| Technical | versus | Process |
| Detail | versus | Concept |
| Patent inventors | versus | Problem solvers |
| Sociable group inventors | versus | 'Lone wolves' |

**Figure 6.1** Classification of the characteristics of inventors.

The most commonly mentioned characteristics of an innovative person include a broad view, a holistic perspective, a tendency to 'think outside the box' and a likelihood to use abstract and conceptual thinking in tasks or projects. They will almost certainly be persistent, willing to learn and show curiosity. They can also be very dedicated and motivated, but on the other hand show streaks of rebelliousness. They will usually prove to be 'serial networkers' as well.

# Recognising and rewarding inventors

This subject has already been raised in Chapter 4 on innovation. However, it is worthwhile revisiting this issue again here, as it is of importance to inventors. Employees make more than 80% of inventions and it is therefore important that the Patent Creation Factory knows its own rights with regard to an invention, as well as the rights of his employees. The general rule is that where an employee creates an invention in the course of his or her employment, this invention and any patent will belong to the employer. However, there are statutory provisions in place to ensure that the employee does not go unrewarded.

Germany and Japan are two examples of jurisdictions where employee compensation is common. German law regulates matters of employee ownership of inventions and the compensation to which they are entitled by statute. Where inventions are made in the course of the employee's duties, the employer may claim them. The employee must give notice to the employer of the making of an invention and allow the employer the option to make a limited or unlimited claim to the invention. In the latter case, the employer is entitled to an assignment but must pay 'reasonable compensation' for this. Similar compensation is due where the employer makes a limited claim, the only difference being that they derive rights to the invention from a non-exclusive licence. The German government has published guidelines to be used when calculating compensation. In essence, inventions that produce high turnover will attract high compensation payments. In Japan, employees are the owners of all inventions they make including those in the course of their duties. Employers often use employment contracts in order to entitle them to ownership over the invention or at the very least an exclusive licence. When an employee assigns his or her invention or grants an exclusive licence to the employer, Japanese Patent Law entitles the employee to reasonable remuneration. This is calculated on the basis of the resulting profits made by the employer from the invention and the contribution to the invention made by the employee. Large Japanese companies often have preset scales of remuneration for employee's inventions.

Most innovative businesses provide rewards and some form of recognition to inventors and yes, there are legal requirements in certain jurisdictions to take into consideration. More importantly, however, a good comprehensive reward and recognition programme encourages and motivates innovation and creativity. The elements of such a programme may include such elements as financial awards but it needs to go beyond this. The recognition element is also important and serious consideration needs to be given to this part of the programme.

# PULL versus PUSH modes of operation

The most important source of raw material for the Patent Creation Factory is the inventor community, and so improving the quantity and quality of ideas that are coming from this community should be of the highest priority for any patent creation group.

Someone needs to invent. Traditionally inventions come from within research and development but the inventor community is much broader than this and increasingly includes people spread throughout the company.

Today, companies cannot survive in isolation. They need to cooperate and collaborate with other companies, universities and external individuals. All these different people must also be recognised as potentially belonging to your inventor community.

The Patent Creation Factory must know and understand the inventor community, how they see patenting and their views on the subject, because this enables you to amend activities in order to reach the desired end result of obtaining inventions. If you are aware of factors that work against your patenting goals and targets, there is a need to develop ways of dealing with and controlling these issues.

Switching from a passive mode to an active mode, or in other words actively seeking out new sources of patents and new patent ideas, also deserves some consideration. How should the Patent Creation Factory approach this task and how should it be decided whether the efforts needed for this mode of operation are going to produce adequate results? How frequently should this task be performed? In recent times a trend is clearly taking place whereby Patent Creation Factories are switching from the passive PUSH mode, where you wait for inventions to be submitted, to the more active PULL mode, where you seek out inventions in key technology areas and from leading edge research and technology and product programmes, but at the same time remain ready and willing to handle 'out of the box' ideas from left field. A trend is also taking place whereby intellectual property experts are working together with the general legal community, as well as the sourcing and purchasing experts within companies, in order to ensure that intellectual property terms and conditions are properly incorporated into contracts with suppliers, vendors and university 'partners'. This includes areas such as idea generation and invention harvesting.

PULL mode activities may include such things as conducting invention workshops on specific areas of interest, actively working with lead technology projects to harvest inventions, working closely with the top inventors and establishing invention targets together with business and technology management.

## Appreciate your inventor community

You need to understand and appreciate your inventor community. Begin by deciding how best to sub-divide or categorise them. Then rate them and finally decide where to focus your time and energy. Understanding and appreciating your raw materials and product components and who is supplying them, is just as important to the Patent Creation Factory as it is to the traditional factory. Without the inventor community, the Patent Creation Factory may as well pack up its bags and go home.

You should therefore look on your inventor community as your key supplier and it is essential that you ensure good relations in order to maintain supply. Communication is the key! At a general level, make sure that your inventors and in particular your top inventors, know and understand the strategy of your Patent Creation Factory. Do they know your targets and do they know who's who in your factory when they wish to discuss an issue or concern? Will your Patent Creation Factory listen to them when they have valid recommendations to make or they raise any issues or concerns. On the case specific level, it is important that a good professional working relationship exists between the inventor and the patent professional responsible for drafting, filing and prosecuting the case through the patenting process. The inventor should be kept informed of progress as the case progresses. If, for any reason, a decision is taken not to progress with the invention through to the patenting process, that decision should also be explained to the inventor. It is most important to remember that just because an idea is not put through to the patenting process, it does not mean that it is not a good idea. The establishment of an appeals process is also worth considering.

Most innovative businesses provide rewards and some form of recognition to inventors. There are two main reasons for having a reward and recognition programme in place for inventors. The first is that there are legal requirements in certain jurisdictions to take into consideration and secondly and more importantly, a good comprehensive reward and recognition program encourages and motivates innovation and creativity.

The components of a programme may include such elements as financial awards, plaques, patent festivals or celebrations and recognition of the inventor by Senior Management. Other small but simple and effective ways to indicate top inventors are top inventor get-togethers and published league tables of the top inventors within the organisation. The value of a simple 'thank you' or 'well done' should also not be overlooked.

> *"Appreciation can make a day, even change a life. Your willingness to put it into word is all that is necessary."* Margaret Cousins

# 7

# Other key interfaces

## Introduction

Apart from the inventor community discussed in Chapter 6, there are a number of other critical interfaces to manage, as well as relationships to develop and maintain, in order to ensure that a patent factory is successful in creating the highest quality patents. Although the primary focus of this book is on the Patent Creation Factory, this chapter again looks outside the factory at these critical groups. There are five key groupings of importance to the patent factory, namely, the inventor community, the senior management of the company, the 'other half' of intellectual property rights (IPR), the business and technology management in the company and the External Patent Agencies/other external IPR organisations and offices (Figure 7.1). Chapter 6 dealt with the inventor community, the vital source of the patent factory's critical raw material, and this chapter addresses the other four important interfaces.

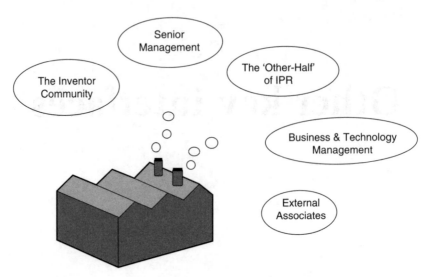

**Figure 7.1** The key external interfaces of a Patent Creation Factory.

> *"The most basic of all human needs is the need to understand and be understood. The best way to understand people is to listen to them."*     Ralph Nichols

## Senior management

Senior management refers to that team of individuals at the highest level of the organisation's management, who take care of the day-to-day responsibilities of managing the company.

I have talked already about the growing strategic importance of intellectual property (IP) and it is clear that the importance of intangible assets is growing, often equalling or surpassing the value of physical assets for a company. The state of the IP of your company can determine your share and corresponding influence on the market. The size and quality of your portfolio has a direct impact on several factors, such as the reputation of your company, the level of return on investments and your access to the market, among others. Your IPR are also a mark of the innovation and creativity within your company. Building and maintaining a patent portfolio requires investment decisions to be made and having and maintaining good quality, valuable IPR open up opportunities for the company.

It is an interesting exercise to highlight some of the language in the paragraph above, such as 'growing strategic importance', 'influence on the market', 'reputation of your company', 'return on investment', 'a mark of innovation and creativity', 'investment decisions' and 'opportunities'. This is the language of senior management and these are the topics one would expect to hear being discussed in the company boardrooms.

It is therefore only natural that an interface of some importance exists between the patent factory and senior management of the company, and this is a critical relationship to be developed and fostered, given the impact that IP has on the issues of concern to senior management.

There are certain attributes needed for a successful interface between senior management and the Patent Creation Factory. Good, honest communication flow in both directions is paramount, as is encouragement by senior management through words and deeds, for innovation and creativity throughout the company. It is important that there is genuine interest and active involvement to some degree by senior management in the world of IP and the Patent Creation Factory. Strategy alignment is needed between the company's overall strategy, the company's IP strategy and the patent factory's strategy/top level action plans. This includes a realistic budget because a Patent Creation Factory will need money to invest in innovation, patent filing and prosecution and the maintenance of a patent portfolio. Other help and support will be needed along the way and possibly the most important attribute will be patience; the patenting process is a relatively long one, particularly when compared to the speed of technology advancement in many industries.

> *"Reactive innovation does little to differentiate a company from the competition, and just delays the sinking of the ship. Innovation must be pervasive and perpetual: everyone, everywhere, all of the time. Innovation must be seen as the key currency within the company."* Stephen Shapiro

The Patent Creation Factory in turn needs to be able to translate the value of the intangible assets associated with IPR and patents into language that senior management understand, such as strategic value, monetary value and/or competitive advantage. This ability to translate or convert intangible asset value into tangible asset value is of critical importance, because without that skill, there may be a serious disconnection between the Patent Creation Factory and senior management.

Senior management may have learnt to repeat the mantra that 'intellectual property is important' but in many companies the meaning is not understood and even in companies where it is understood by some, you will still see some senior managers' eyes glaze over when talk turns to IP and patent issues. The opposite challenge sometimes applies to IP professionals as they may tend to become so specialised in the intricacies of patentability and intellectual property law that they do not really understand the business and customer needs, product development, profit margins and other business issues.

# The 'other half' of IPR

The 'other half' of IPR refers to those who utilise the patents in one way or another, after the Patent Creation Factory has created the patents. It typically means those involved with the licensing of IP, but it may also include those involved with technology transfer activities, cooperation and collaboration agreements with third parties, standardisation activities, university relations, mergers and acquisitions and litigation, i.e., basically anyone who utilises the intangible assets obtained by the patent factory in order to obtain some return on their investment.

For many companies and organisations, the 'other half' of IPR refers to those involved with the licensing of IP. It is important, when a factory is producing patents, that these patents are suited to the negotiations of the licensing group, both at the present time and in the distant future. The key factor here therefore is that there must be an alignment between what is being produced and what is demanded. A factory should only produce a product in the knowledge that it is satisfying some sort of demand.

Another key role played by the licensing group is that it can provide valuable feedback to the patent factory in relation to the quality of a patent. If a patent is not good quality, that is, it cannot be enforced, the licensing group must provide the information as to why this is so. Clearly, this is important because feedback from the licensing group should allow you to improve the quality of your patents.

The Patent Creation Factory also needs to have a good understanding and appreciation of how the various patents that it is creating are actually being utilised. What is the IP landscape in your industry for your company and how is the IP game being played? What is the playing field and who are the players? What are the possible IP conflicts, and are there some limitations or constraints in place in this 'IP game'? You will need to examine the risks.

The same attributes needed for a successful interface between senior management and the Patent Creation Factory also apply to the 'other half' of IPR. Good, honest communication flow in both directions is again paramount, and a genuine interest and active involvement by the IP people involved in licensing and litigation, back down to the floor of the Patent Creation Factory. Strategy alignment is needed between the company's overall strategy, the company's IP strategy and the Patent Creation Factory's strategic top-level action plans. Feedback on the quality of patents being obtained and a good understanding of how the 'IP game' is being played will also be needed. Patent Creation Factory target setting should be an exercise conducted together with the 'other half' of IPR (Table 7.1).

**Table 7.1** Patent Creation Factory targets for new filings

| Technology area | Filing targets | |
| | Target | Rationale |
| --- | --- | --- |
| Area #1 | 5 | |
| Area #2 | 15 | New technology focus area |
| Area #3 | 12 | |
| Area #4 | 3 | Strong portfolio in place |

# Business and technology management

Business management refers to those involved with the design and development of the products and services of interest to the company, and the marketing, distribution and selling of said items. Technology management refers to those involved in the research and development or in the procurement of the core technologies needed to design and develop the products and services above. These departments identify what these key core technologies, products and services are today and what they may be in the future.

There must be some alignment between the ideas behind the technologies, products features, product functions and services coming into the patent factory and those in which the company is most interested and actually involved with, as it goes about its core business.

This alignment allows the factory to relate to the appropriate inventors and the owners of the technology of the company, and furthermore it enables them to draft road maps that symbolise what they hope to achieve in future. This beneficial arrangement then helps to determine the focus of the factory manager.

Earlier in this section, the phrase 'some alignment' was used rather than just the word 'alignment'. This was deliberate because a good patent creation factory should not be 100% aligned with the core technologies, product features and functions and services of the company. You need some unalignment to allow for ideas coming from 'left field' and for ideas that are not in your company's roadmaps but may be in others.

Once again, some of the attributes needed for a successful interface between senior management and the Patent Creation Factory also apply to the business and technology managers within the company. Good, honest communication flow in both directions is again paramount, as is encouragement by senior management through words and deeds, for innovation and creativity throughout the company. It is important that there is a genuine interest and active involvement to some degree by business and technology managers back down to the floor of the Patent Creation Factory. There will also need to be some alignment between the company's technology and product roadmaps and the patent factory's strategy and top-level action plans. You will also need to incorporate IP targets into the technology, product and services projects of the company. And again, business and technology management have to be involved to some degree with target setting for the Patent Creation Factory.

# External Patent Agencies and other IP organisations

External Patent Agencies will be addressed in greater detail in Chapter 9, but the key point is that these agencies need to be involved in patent creation, because not everything can be done in-house.

There are intellectual property or patent specific companies capable of handling parts of or all the tasks of a Patent Creation Factory on your behalf. Their capabilities range from analysis of the novelty and patentability of an idea through to actual drafting of cases, filing the appropriate paperwork with the patent offices, prosecution cases including handling office actions, doing translation work, filing foreign cases with the appropriate patent offices, conducting detailed searches and examinations; basically all tasks right up until the grant stage. There are also external companies who will manage the payment of annuity fees on your behalf.

Involving External Patent Agencies into the operation of your Patent Creation Factory basically means buying certain work results from third parties. Subcontract work is normally based on your specifications and requirements, but you, being the customer and the external patent agencies may also compile specifications together. This is indeed a better approach as it allows the External Patent Agencies to contribute based on their skills, competencies and knowledge.

The patent factory can do a lot of things itself but certain aspects will need to be dealt with externally. It is therefore of great important that you grow and develop a great relationship with these External Patent Agencies.

# Summary

The patent factory should not, and cannot, exist in isolation. This chapter looked at some key entities that are outside the Patent Creation Factory but of critical importance to its success.

Now, depending on the scale of your particular patent factory, the organisational model you adopt, the processes you put in place and the nature of your company's business, plus probably a number of other factors, your patent factory's external interfaces may be slightly different from what is described here.

Regardless, you will have a number of critical external interfaces to manage, and relationships to develop and maintain, in order to ensure that your patent factory is successful in creating good quality and valuable patents. Communication will be the key to your success.

> *"I know you believe you understand what you think I said, but I'm not sure you realise that what you heard is not what I meant."*    Robert McCloskey

You will need to identify the external interfaces that exist in your particular case, gain insight and understanding of each of these interfaces, and determine what is needed to make all these interfaces work well. It is also worth noting that your external interfaces will very likely change over time thanks perhaps to company level organisational changes, IP level organisational changes, changes to your patent factory strategy and top-level action plans or changes happening in the external world.

# 8

# Organising your patent factory

IN THE PREVIOUS CHAPTERS, I HIGHLIGHTED THE MANY
issues that need to be considered and handled by a Patent
Creation Factory. I stressed the growing strategic importance of patents and encouraged you to start with a strategy
and an action plan, followed by a thorough study and analysis
of your primary interfaces.

Now the question is, how are you going to organise and structure your internal Patent Creation Factory in an effective and
efficient manner?

This chapter outlines the factors that you need to consider
when deciding how to organise, structure and operate the
patent factory. It provides examples of organisation models,
including diagrams, which outline possible ways to organise,
plus techniques to overcome issues and problems that may
arise.

The selection and deployment of the structure and mode of operation of the Patent Creation Factory should not be made randomly. There are choices to be made, and this chapter explains the factors that need to be taken into account, so that you can decide the organisation structure that best suits your specific situation.

# Key factors to consider

What are the factors to consider as you set about organising your Patent Creation Factory? It is important to ask yourself this because there are some fundamental questions to answer that will really affect and impact the organisation model selection. In my opinion, the fundamental factors to consider are as follows:

- your company's strategies and in particular the intellectual property activities; that is, where you are today and where you hope to be in the future;

- your inventor community, and PULL versus PUSH approaches (see Chapter 6);

- your other key interfaces and how they are organised and structured;

- your business environment and the competitive pressures you face;

- your Patent Creation Factory personnel;

- your key core processes.

The most successful organisations focus the activities and energy of all their resources on key strategic deliverables.

There was a time when organisations could succeed even though they were unaligned and semi-dysfunctional, but those times are rapidly disappearing. The organisations that succeed today are those that can convey a clear vision, focus their resources on the key strategic deliverables and live by a well defined set of values.

> *"It is not the strongest of the species that survive, nor the most intelligent, but the one most responsive to change."* Charles Darwin

Innovative and creative ideas are the raw material of your patent factory and the quality of your ideas therefore has a direct outcome on the success of what you have set out to achieve. It is therefore important that you not only ensure that your ideas are of the highest quality, but also that there is a steady supply of them in order to create a patent portfolio. It is also important to realise that ideas may come from many sources. The inventor community is the collection of individuals who supply the innovation, creativity and ideas, which act as the basic raw materials in the patent factory. There is, however, not one homogenous community of inventors (see Chapter 6). Just as any traditional factory needs to understand and appreciate the source, volume, quality and logistics of the raw materials and product components being supplied into their factory, the very same applies to our patent factory. The interface to your inventor community is therefore something that needs to be taken into consideration as you go about defining your organisational model and mode of operation.

Apart from the inventor community, there are some other key entities outside of the patent creation factory that are of critical importance to its success. You will therefore have a number of critical external interfaces to manage and relationships to develop and maintain, in order to ensure that your patent factory is successful in creating good quality and valuable patents. You will need to identify the external interfaces existing in your particular case, gain insight and understanding of each of these interfaces, and determine what is needed to make all these interfaces work well. The interfaces to all these entities are therefore something that need to be considered.

Your business environment and competitive landscape should impact the organisational model and mode of operation you select and deploy. How much money do you have at your disposal to run a Patent Creation Factory and how does your patent portfolio compare and contrast with your key competitors? How stable is your business and your industry and is your company thinking strategically and long term?

The old saying that 'people are your most important asset' is very true. Many organisations are obsessed with the customer. They are focused on accelerating growth and profitability by attracting new customers, retaining existing customers, deepening customer relationships and providing customer satisfaction. There is absolutely nothing wrong with that approach but organisations should also have an obsession with creating engaged, passionate, skilled and competent employees. The Patent Creation Factory is no different and the organisational model you select needs to be the one that empowers your own people.

> *"Those who perform love what they are doing."*
> Peter Drucker

The process to get from idea to granted patent is fundamental to your Patent Creation Factory. In our factory, it is the equivalent of starting out with the raw materials and step-by-step watching a different part of your product being assembled. At the end of this process you will have your fully assembled product, that is, you will have your patent. The activities of our factory are effectively the same no matter which process you choose. However, there are certain advantages to each procedure depending upon the nature of your invention and the scope of the protection you seek. Each route also requires of you small differences and it is therefore useful to consider each core activity individually.

You may decide that you want to protect your inventions only in your own country or maybe a few others, in which case the simplest route is just to apply to the national offices of the countries in which you want to have protection. Should you decide that you wish to extend your protection to a geographic area, spanning more than several countries, the regional route will prove most suitable. Finally, should you desire to have protection of a more international scope, the Patent Cooperation Treaty (PCT) caters for this alternative. (See Chapter 5 for more details on these options.) So your national, regional and/or global filing strategy will impact the organisational model and definitely the mode of operation of your Patent Creation Factory.

# Organisational models to consider

> *"Every company has two organisation structures, the formal one is written on the charts, the other is the everyday relationship of the men and women in the organisation."*  Harold S. Geneen

There are indeed a variety of organisational models that you can select and there are pros and cons associated with each model. The models are not by any means mutually exclusive, and it may well be that the organisation model you select consists of elements of more than one of the models illustrated below. There may also be other organisation models worth considering that are not presented here.

The organisational models to be examined are as follows:

- by steps in the filing and prosecution process;

- by business unit or division;

- 100% outsourced;

- by location;

- a mix of internal and external;

- by portfolio;

- as a resource pool;

- file everything approach;

- by technology;

- patent acquisitions approach;

- indemnification approach.

## By steps in the filing and prosecution process

This organisation model is based on mapping the structure of the Patent Creation Factory most closely to the key steps in the filing and prosecution process (Figure 8.1); that is, the core activities of the patent factory as described in Chapter 5.

With this model you are able to build up a team of experts in the very specific phases of the patenting process and have a dedicated group in place to gather inventions. It allows you to choose selectively the most efficient party to do the work in the different phases. With this model it is easy to identify which tasks to outsource and which tasks should be kept in-house, and then it is relatively simple to implement such a change. This model also allows you to become very efficient in the volume game.

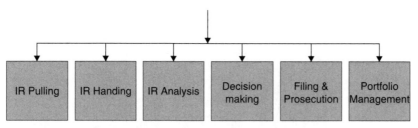

**Figure 8.1** Organising your patent factory by steps in the filing and prosecution process.

However, there are a lot of interfaces to manage, and you may find you are resource heavy with say, six persons needed to study and understand a case instead of only one or two. Usually patent attorneys like to cover the full spectrum of the patenting process, and so there is a danger of de-motivated staff, as no one will have an overall view. This model may also be difficult to implement if the team is not co-located and quality will be dependent on the weakest link in the chain.

## By business unit or division

The Patent Creation Factory here aligns its organisation model very much with the organisational model that the company has adopted, by sub-dividing the factory so as to match the various business units or divisions within the company (Figure 8.2).

This model should provide good buy-in from the business units as they have dedicated support and this allows close cooperation and even integration with the individual business units. If the business units within a company are very different in nature, the model allows the patent factory to be different when it best suits, which may be the case if you have

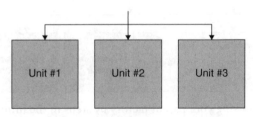

**Figure 8.2**   Organising your patent factory by business unit or division.

acquired different companies or have differing cultures and diverse intellectual property rights (IPR) backgrounds.

The drawbacks may be a lack of consistency between the units, and the patent factory may have to re-organise and change whenever the business units change. You will need to work out how to enable efficient communication between the business units to prevent duplication of work and also be aware of the danger of 'silos' developing.

## 100% outsourced

As the name suggests, this model proposes that you outsource all activities of the Patent Creation Factory, leaving only a small core team internally to coordinate activities between the groups illustrated (Figure 8.3).

This is a good model if headcount is an issue, because costs can be kept low by outsourcing to inexpensive

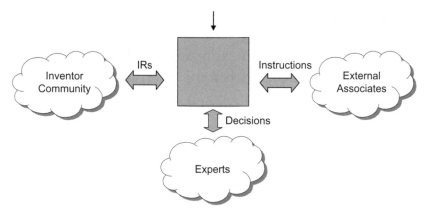

**Figure 8.3** Organising your patent factory by outsourcing 100% of the activities.

locations. The company would also have access to experienced attorneys and the benefits of training from these experienced attorneys.

However, excellent outsourcing management skills are needed to determine that the external resources are performing well, because it takes time, energy and skill to manage third parties properly. There is always a possibility that the external attorneys may have a lack of understanding of the company's strategy and technology, which will result in low 'business' quality of the patent applications. Also, internal technical experts may not be comfortable dealing with external attorneys, or vice versa.

## By location

The Patent Creation Factory here aligns its organisation model very much with the physical locations where the company has presence, or perhaps where research and development activities take place, sub-dividing the factory so as to match this set-up (Figure 8.4).

With this model, you can easily adapt to local and cultural needs and there is usually better support for the local units

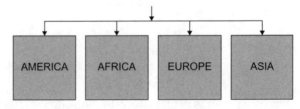

**Figure 8.4**  Organising your patent factory by physical location.

and local inventors. This can also be an efficient model in foreign filing and it can be relatively easy to create close links with external third parties.

With this organisation model, however, you are reliant on a good network of contacts between sites to keep consistency. When the network of contacts breaks down, this can lead to a lack of consistency between sites over a period of time. It is important to ensure that all teams have a basic understanding of requirements in the different regions as this will help prevent disharmony between the units. There may be challenges with recruitment in some locations and resource levels may not always match needs at local sites. This model may not suit a company that thinks globally, as local laws might be an issue from a global point of view.

## A mix of internal and external

It is important to realise that just as with modern factories, not all the tasks and activities are handled internally by the factory's own employees or even by the key suppliers and component vendors. Some tasks are outsourced to specialists and this model suggests that you give serious consideration to having some activities done by such external specialists; the division between internal and external is the critical one as far as your organisational model is concerned (Figure 8.5).

Internal skills are available to monitor the performance of externals; resource management is more flexible and allows learning and knowledge transfer between one another. Cases

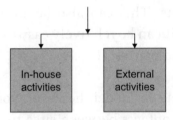

**Figure 8.5**  Organising your patent factory by a mix of internal and external activities.

can be divided, for example with urgent or critical cases handled internally and others handled externally. It should be noted that internal is not automatically better and sometimes you get better quality from externals. This model also gives the Patent Creation factory the opportunity to offer more diverse tasks to the internal workforce.

Excellent outsourcing management skills, however, are needed to determine that the external resources are performing well, because it takes time, energy and skill to manage third parties properly. And again, there is the possibility that the external attorneys may lack understanding of your company's strategy and technology.

## By portfolio

Here, the assumption is that you have a patent portfolio already in place and that it needs managing in terms of understanding what rights you have accumulated (Figure 8.6). You also need to identify the areas of strengths, taking concrete steps to address areas of weakness and converting this patent portfolio into true value for the company.

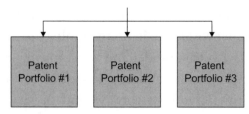

**Figure 8.6** Organising your patent factory by portfolio.

The solution is to focus more on managing and improving an existing portfolio rather than building a portfolio from scratch and this model supports the target setting when focus and prioritisation is needed when creating patents.

On the other hand, attorneys may not be familiar with the division of work into Filing and Prosecution tasks and Patent Portfolio Management tasks. This model may also create a lack of understanding between the portfolios and there may be difficulties in mapping certain cases to one specific patent portfolio.

## As a resource pool

This model treats your Patent Creation Factory personnel as a resource pool with no real organisation structure in place other than the pool itself (Figure 8.7).

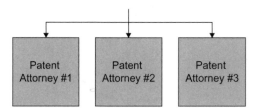

**Figure 8.7** Organising your patent factory by resource pool.

This model is ideal if resource management is your key issue of concern. However, there is no technology focus by individual attorneys with this model and work may become random in nature, with a lack of synergy. It almost certainly reduces the need for initiative by attorneys and there will be a lack of contact between attorneys and business and technology units.

## File everything approach

As the name suggests, this model is based on letting your External Patent Agencies determine which of the cases they wish to progress through the patenting process based on some pre-determined and agreed criteria (Figure 8.8).

This model is similar in many ways to the 100 % outsourced approach described earlier, with many of the same pros and cons that are listed there.

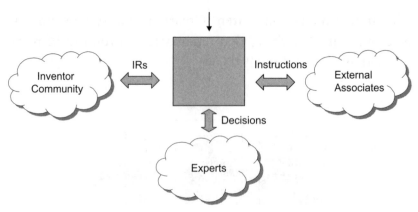

**Figure 8.8**  Organising your patent factory by the file everything approach.

There are no internal resource issues to worry about, because the need for internal resources is kept to a minimum.

This model is expensive to support but it allows a quick growth of the patent portfolio, although the quality of the patents may be suspect. You are dependent on external attorneys and patent offices to filter 'the good from the bad'.

## By technology area

The Patent Creation Factory here aligns its organisation model very much with the key technologies and areas of interest in which the company has a presence, or perhaps where it has key research and development activities taking place (Figure 8.9). It does this by sub-dividing the factory so as to match the set-up.

This model promotes good links with the key technology projects and allows the patent factory to work closely with the key technologists and build up long-term relationships. This promotes strong links between the key inventors and IPR. Based on our own benchmarking exercise, this is a fairly common organisational model in many Patent Creation Factories.

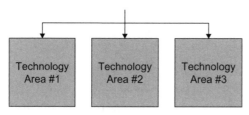

**Figure 8.9** Organising your patent factory by technical area.

There can, however, be a very real danger of missing 'blue sky' research ideas if they are outside the selected technology areas, so it is very important to define a strategy to work with the new and emerging technologies. It may become a challenge to ensure that the 'business inventions', which are not so technologically advanced, get through to the patenting stage.

## Patent acquisitions approach

This model completely skips over the invention harvesting approach and proposes a model where patents are acquired from others so as to develop a patent portfolio for the company (Figure 8.10).

This model is a patent buying system in which the granted patent is more valuable than the invention report. If there is no real research and development taking place internally, and there are critical gaps in your research and development activities, this is good approach. Such an organisation would proactively seek interesting patent acquisition opportunities and then manage any resultant transaction that may result. It may also work in cooperation with others such as mergers

**Figure 8.10** Organising your patent factory by the patent acquisitions approach.

and acquisitions experts if a mergers and acquisitions initiative was IPR driven.

However, this may be an expensive model and you still need support from IPR experts to understand what you are buying. Your success is also very dependent on what others, completely outside of your control, have done already with respect to the filing of patent applications.

This model may therefore work parallel to other models suggested, to complete an organisational model.

## Indemnification approach

This model is based on the concept of obtaining indemnifications from others to allow you to conduct your business without worrying about patents (Figure 8.11).

This approach may be useful if you are just assembling or utilising technologies coming from key suppliers. It is a very simple model and extremely cost effective, although it can be risky. The model is dependent on the patent strength of

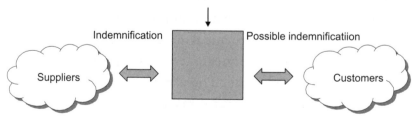

**Figure 8.11** Organising your patent factory by the indemnification approach.

others and if you decide to change your business strategy you will have no existing patent portfolio.

As discussed above, there are indeed a large variety of organisational structures from which to select and advantages and disadvantages are associated with each and every one. No single structure is the clear winner and it needs to be stressed that the structures described are not by any means mutually exclusive. It may well be that the organisation structure you select consists of elements of two or more of the structures illustrated above. The organisational structure that best suits your circumstances today may not be the best option for you in the future, as your patent creation factory develops and matures, and so it is almost certain that your organisational structure will change over time. There may also be other organisation structures worth considering that have not been presented here.

## Organisational change

You should not change just for the sake of change! There is typically a strong resistance to change within companies because people are afraid of change or rather the 'unknown' that change brings. Many of your people may believe that things are working just fine and do not understand the need for change. Many may be cynical about change, or doubt that there are more effective means to accomplish your goals, than those already in place. There may be conflicting goals, for example a wish to increase resources to accomplish the strategic objectives and yet concurrently a pressure to cut costs in order to remain viable. Organisational change may go against the values of the company, that is, the change may be contradictory to how some of your people believe things should be done.

Conducting a major organisational change should therefore only be done if it is a fundamental part of your strategy to accomplish your overall goal. Some major force usually drives organisational change, and pressure to change your organisational model and mode of operation may come from one or more of a number of sources. Pressure from the top may manifest itself in a number of ways and you may find yourself being asked a number of questions. Can your strategy be implemented with the current organisational structure and mode of operation? Is your business environment changing so much that although it is working fine today, your current model will not work well in the future? How well does your model align with the organisational model and mode of operation of the rest of your company? Pressure to change may also come from within. How are you performing when measured against your own current metrics and what would a SWOT (Strengths, Weaknesses, Opportunities and Threats) assessment of your current Patent Creation Factory tell you? What are your own employees telling you via, for example, employee opinion surveys? How effective and efficient are your current Patent Creation Factory processes and do you have the skills and competencies needed within your factory to succeed? A red flag indicating that all is not well and that some change is needed, may come from outside your Patent Creation Factory. What feedback are you getting from your key 'customers and suppliers' about your service level and performance and how is your relationship with your inventor community? Most importantly how satisfied is the 'other half' of IPR with the patent portfolio you are creating?

> *"Change is the law of life. And those who look only to the past or present are certain to miss the future."*
> John F. Kennedy

You should only consider conducting an organisational change when you have satisfied yourself that you have answers to the three fundamental questions: where are we now?; where do we want to be?; and how are we going to get there?

Change management is a structured approach to change in individuals or organisations that enables the transition from the present state to a desired future state. From an individual perspective, the change may be a related to behaviour but from an organisational perspective the change may be a new structure and mode of operation. Successful change requires much more than a new organisation chart or new process description. It requires the active engagement and participation of all the people involved.

Any successful change must involve senior management. Usually there will be a change 'champion' who initially instigates the change by being visionary, persuasive and consistent. However this vision then needs to be translated into a realistic plan. Organisational change is best carried out as a team-wide effort and communication about the change should be frequent and should reach everyone who will be impacted. To sustain change, the structures of the organisation itself should be modified, including strategic plans, policies and procedures. This change in the structures typically involves an unfreezing stage before the change or changes can take place, followed by a refreezing process. The best approach to address resistance is through increased and sustained communication and education. The leader of the change project needs to explain to all the people impacted the reasons for the change, give general information on how the changes will be carried out and ensure that people know where they can find additional information on how the changes will affect them. Your initial plan needs to be developed and communicated and, going forward, needs to incorporate any changes to the project. Whenever your original plan changes you should always communicate this to your people and explain the reasons for the change to the plan. Meetings should be arranged for the people impacted to allow them to express their ideas and opinions on the planned changes and be prepared for them to express their concerns and frustrations as well.

Creating a meaningful and lasting change in strategy, operational structure and mode of operation that results in improved competitiveness, effectiveness and efficiency is not just about management but is first and foremost about leadership. Real change involves changing behaviours as well as improving systems and procedures because effective change involves an understanding of organisational values and culture and, in particular, the strengths and weaknesses. Thus, values and culture can be an organisation's greatest strength when they are consistent with its strategy and mode of operation. However, a culture that prevents an organisation from addressing competitive threats or from adapting to changing environments, can lead to the organisation's stagnation and ultimate collapse.

Successful change requires detailed knowledge of the way your organisation functions, an honest appraisal of its strengths and weaknesses and an assessment of how performance will be affected by change.

## Summary

Research indicates that the role of leadership in times of transition is changing. It is moving away from being reactive, towards a much more proactive change management role and the creation of more flexible and networked organisational structures.

Successful organisations focus the activities and energy of all their resources on key strategic deliverables. There was a time when organisations could succeed without such issues being considered, but those times are rapidly disappearing. The organisations that succeed today are those that can convey a clear vision, focus their resources on the key strategic deliverables and live by a well-defined set of values.

> *"Business success is a function of fit between a host of key variables within an organization ... strategy, values, culture, employees, systems, organizational design and the behaviour of the senior management team all have to be in alignment."* Michael Beer

Being a true Patent Creation Factory leader today means acting as a change agent to align people and strategy for organisational excellence. You must develop skills and competencies and learn new ways of assessing appropriate operational focus, while developing strategic long-term direction and leveraging both financial and human resources that will promote organisational effectiveness and financial performance.

This involves assessing your organisation's vision and the translation of your strategic intent into action. You need to grow and develop your people; roles and responsibilities must be well defined, yet offer some degree of flexibility. Team building procedures and methods should be well understood and be an integral part of your mode of operation, and you must ensure that motivation and reward systems are in place. Implementing such change may mean enacting the organisational model in a regional or global environment and not just at a local level.

There are a variety of organisational models to select for your Patent Creation Factory and I have described a number of such models in this chapter. There are advantages and disadvantages associated with each model. The models are by no means mutually exclusive and it may well be that the organisation model you select consists of elements of more than one of the models. In addition, there may well be other organisation models worth considering.

> *"When you're finished changing you're finished."*
> Benjamin Franklin

# 9

# The management of External Patent Agencies

## Who are the External Patent Agencies and what services do they provide?

When we examined Patent Creation Factory organisational models in the previous chapter, there were many options highlighted, some of which involved doing some of the work outside the walls of your factory. In fact, a few of the models suggested outsourcing all or almost all the activities of your Patent Creation Factory.

There are indeed intellectual property (IP) or patent specific companies capable of handling parts of or all the tasks of a Patent Creation Factory on your behalf. Their capabilities range from analysis of the novelty and patentability of an idea, through to actual drafting of cases, filing the appropriate paperwork with the patent offices, prosecution of cases, and handling office actions and taking care of translation work. Also included would be filing foreign cases with the appropriate patent offices, conducting detailed searches and examinations and all tasks right up until the grant stage. There are also external companies who will manage the payment of annuity fees on your behalf.

The term External Patent Agency is used throughout the book to describe these IP or patent companies. They are sometimes referred to as Patent Agencies, Patent Firms or Patent Attorney Firms. Some general law firms may have some Patent Attorneys or Patent Agents working within the company, who focus on IP or patent issues, and a simple Internet search will display this kind of information of available patent agencies. Most of these External Patent Agencies have web sites or publications available, where they advertise their contact details and the services offered.

## Why subcontract?

Involving an External Patent Agency into the operation of your Patent Creation Factory basically means buying certain work results from third parties. Subcontract work is normally based on your specifications and requirements but you, being the customer, and the External Patent Agency may also compile specifications together. This is indeed a better approach as it allows the External Patent Agency to contribute based on its skills, competencies and knowledge.

There are many reasons to subcontract work to an External Patent Agency. Outsourcing may increase your flexibility in terms of resourcing, leading to faster response times and wider overall opportunities when your competence and capacity pool is expanded through these External Patent Agencies. You may wish to focus your limited resources on what you consider to be core activities, critical cases or in key competence areas. Outsourcing may provide you with market making opportunities or provide you with access to new markets, which would be more difficult or impossible without the external relationship. It may also provide you access to proprietary competencies or give you access to new competencies faster than trying to develop such competencies in-house.

Various business models may be used to define the nature of the working relationship between you and the External Patent Agencies. Your business model may be outsourcing, where you transfer an activity to an External Patent Agency, who then continue to provide this activity to you as one of its customers. Your business model may be more akin to external temporary labour, where you buy a short-term external workforce from an External Patent Agency, to work on your specific assignment. Or, it may be subcontracting, where you purchase predefined deliverables from an External Patent Agency. A specific sub-stream of subcontracting is called service provision, which means the purchase of a pre-defined end service from a provider, according to certain service level specifications. This business model should also specify terms and conditions and a payment plan, between yourself and the External Patent Agency. Pricing and payment may be based on hourly rate(s), which vary according to the skills or qualifications of the person providing the relevant tasks, or on a fixed monthly fee, which would be more applicable in a fairly stable service provisioning environment or according to a very specific pricing model.

## What work can be subcontracted?

Basically, part of or all the tasks of a typical Patent Creation Factory can be subcontracted to External Patent Agencies. The capabilities and duties of the external agent range from analysis of the invention idea for novelty and patentability, through to actual drafting of cases. This includes filing the appropriate paperwork with the patent offices, prosecution of cases, including handling office actions, doing translation work, filing foreign cases with the appropriate patent offices and conducting detailed searches and examinations: basically, all the tasks that fall under the umbrella of 'Patent Creation' right up until the grant stage. Once you have your granted patents, you can also contract an external company to manage the payment of annuity fees on your behalf.

## Challenges in subcontracting

Subcontracting work to an external company is not always easy and there are a number of potential challenges that you need to take into consideration. The contract between you and the External Patent Agency is of paramount importance. There may be no agreement in place, the agreement may be out of date or there may be several agreements in place; even if there is a valid agreement in place, it may not be well written and comprehensive enough to meet your needs. You must also ensure that your practices and those of the External Patent Agency are in line with the agreement.

The pricing arrangements may not be unified, in the sense that there may not be common understanding on pricing, due to a lack of clarity, a lack of detail, or both. When considering costs, you also need to consider the additional costs relating to the management of External Patent Agencies, because this is often ignored.

You should consider whether any challenges exist with the External Patent Agency to whom you wish to outsource work. For example, it may be a small company with a predominant amount of its business coming from you and may have ex-employees of yours working for them. Or the External Patent Agency may be gaining a determining position in that particular market, making it difficult to negotiate. There may also be customer service issues, such as with the timing of due deliverables, cost efficiency, security and confidentiality issues, or possibly the quality of work. Your satisfaction level with the External Patent Agency, and the mutual satisfaction level of both parties, is most important because trust is needed on both sides of the relationship.

# Cooperation with External Patent Agencies

The long-term goal is to have an optimised number of carefully selected External Patent Agencies that are managed in a unified way and with whom the relationship is constantly developing. To ensure that you are managing and developing these relationships, it is worthwhile putting some fundamental elements in place. Professional agreements must be in place between you and your External Patent Agencies and instructions need to be issued to clarify how work tasks are to be ordered. The workflow between you and the External Patent Agencies also needs management, and cost and quality controls need to be put in place.

# Key principles regarding agreements with External Patent Agencies

Having written agreements in place between you and the External Patent Agencies helps clarify the division of responsibilities between the parties, and also serves as a risk management tool.

Such formal agreements may govern the entire relationship or be case specific and the choice here is probably influenced by the volume of work involved, including whether the assignments will be regular or irregular, the criticality of the External Patent Agency in terms of their geographical location and their technical capabilities or capacity.

The following list contains the content that you may wish to consider including within such an agreement with an External Patent Agency. The list is not meant to be exhaustive but hopefully gives you guidance on the creation of a meaningful and valuable agreement.

- **Purpose and scope of the Agreement:** scope of supply of the External Patent Agency, why the agreement is made, what is the general description of the services to be provided by the external Patent Agency and the expected work results.

- **Performance of the Assignment:** items such as (including but not limited to):

  - general quality requirements;

  - resources and equipment provided by both parties;

  - insurances (what insurances are needed/recommended by the customer);

  - version control and security copy (how and how often these should be created by the External Patent Agency, any specific software required by the customer);

  - data privacy: important especially when personal data is transferred to or from EU;

  - changes: how should these be handled, who is responsible for tracking, when and how changes resulting from customer's actions should be taken into account in performing the assignment;

  - status reports: how, how often and to whom should these be delivered;

  - ordering individual assignments: will separate orders be issued, is there a template or a tool used for these, who can order, does the external Patent Agency need to give an order confirmation.

- **Handling conflicts of interest:** what situations might lead to a conflict; how should the customer be informed, should/could, e.g., Chinese walls be created to resolve potential conflicts.

- **Delivery and acceptance of work results:** how work results should be delivered (format, delivery address, etc.); does the customer have an acceptance procedure and is there a fixed timeline for this; how should the External Patent Agency handle any errors that are detected during the acceptance procedure.

- **Quality requirements:** general instructions regarding quality, possible warranty clauses; also detailed quality guidelines can be attached to the agreement, or they can be issued separately.

- **Remedies in case of failure/non-performance/delays:** what actions will the External Patent Agency take when it underperforms or fails to meet the requirements of the customer and/or breaches the agreement, and what sanctions (e.g., monetary) the customer can impose upon the External Patent Agency, for example when delivery is delayed.

- **External Patent Agency's responsibilities as an employer:** emphasis on the fact that the External Patent Agency has ultimate responsibilities for its employees participation in assignments under the agreement, even though the customer has responsibility for management of individual assignments.

- **Prices and terms of payment:** information about the rates and how long they are valid; what information should each invoice contain; invoicing address and other such details if these do not need to be specified in the order form; terms of payment; explanation about how taxes are handled (default is that both parties take care of relevant tax items as stipulated in the relevant legislation).

- **Liability/Indemnification:** what legal consequences and/ or possible monetary damages will the External Patent Agency incur, e.g., if they breach third party intellectual property rights (IPR) when performing the assignment(s).

- **Force Majeure:** what situations fulfil the Force Majeure definition (e.g., war, acts of government, natural disasters) and how would such situations affect the performance of assignments?

- **Confidentiality:** what information is to be considered confidential and how should such information be handled. The confidentiality responsibilities may be mutual or affect only the External Patent Agency.

- **Term and termination of the agreement:** how long the agreement remains valid; how/when/on what grounds the customer and the External Patent Agency can terminate.

The agreement content outlined above is fairly generic and should be adaptable to work for many companies and organisations with ease. Also, the items are not really intellectual property or patent specific, with the only exception perhaps being the conflict of interest topic, which is very much IPR specific. Care needs to be taken how this is handled with an External Patent Agency because in many countries Restrictive Trade Practices legislation is in place.

For many External Patent Agencies the most problematic sections of the agreement tend to be with the following:

- **Quality requirements:** it is a challenge to define adequate or appropriate quality for the drafting and filing of patent applications.

- **Remedies:** the External Patent Agencies may not be used to these with other clients and your quality guidelines and other instructions in the past may not have been unambiguous.

- **Liabilities/Indemnification:** the External Patent Agency's responsibility and possible blame for third party IPR breaches may have been difficult to define, when their entire assignment is about creating new IPR for you.

# Example of a pricing model for External Patent Agency work

It is worthwhile giving consideration to establishing some key pricing principles when you outsource work to External Patent Agencies. Do you wish to keep your pricing structure as simple as possible and to have a similar pricing model that will apply across all your External Patent Agencies? It is most useful if your actual costs follow your budget for each phase of the patenting process. It is also extremely useful if you can estimate costs for drafting, prosecution, foreign filing and annuities and that your pricing model supports this. Lastly, do not forget to include official fees in your figures.

Your pricing model may wish to drill down to agreed fixed prices for items such as the hourly rate for attorney and administrative work, setting a cap or maximum price for draft work expense and setting a cap or maximum price for prosecution expenses. You may also wish to establish fixed fees for administrative tasks that are repeated for (almost) all applications. These administrative tasks may vary from one jurisdiction to another, but can include such tasks as filing, reporting an office action, publication, reporting a grant or reporting an issue. If translation work is involved, you may wish to set a per word rate for certain language pairs, such as English–Chinese. Many External Patent Agencies typically have different hourly rates based on the status of the person in questions (partner, patent agency, junior patent agency, paralegal, etc.).

# Managing the External Patent Agencies

Having formal agreements and pricing models in place with your External Patent Agencies is really only setting the foundation of your working relationship. Much more is needed to truly manage your External Patent Agencies and to establish long-term mutually beneficial professional working relationships.

If you already have or are working to create a relatively large patent portfolio, with a presence across a number of jurisdictions, you more than likely already have dealings with a relatively large number of External Patent Agencies. The creation and maintenance of a global list of approved External Patent Agencies is therefore important, not just as an internal reference list, but so that you can share this with all your External Patent Agencies because they need to know the other agencies on your approved list. Having a global list of approved External Patent Agencies is absolutely necessary if you wish to control which patent attorneys are used in every relevant country. The other alternative may be that you select only the managing or drafting patent agencies and they are then free to use whichever local patent agency they wish. One reason to retain control of each patent agency used is to ensure that conflict of interests issues are handled to your satisfaction.

You will need to gain a good understanding of both the IP and technical skills and competencies of the External Patent Agencies and especially of those individuals within the External Patent Agencies who are actually handling your cases.

Capacity planning together with External Patent Agencies is another important element in your management of them. You need to know how much work the External Patent Agency is willing and able to do for you in the foreseeable future and most importantly if there are any resource issues on the horizon.

External Patent Agencies play a critical role in protecting the intangible assets of your company and it is therefore important that steps are taken to share information with the External Patent Agencies who are drafting, filing and prosecuting your patent applications. Information sharing should extend to providing good quality information about your company, about your strategy, about your Patent Creation Factory targets and about your competitive situation.

How you share this information deserves some thought and consideration, if you want it to add real value to your relationship with your agencies.

To help ensure consistency across your patent portfolio, it is worthwhile creating a requirement specification document or a quality guidelines document, for use by all the patent agents and attorneys who will be drafting, filing and prosecuting patents on your behalf. The goal of such guidelines is to provide some level of consistency in the drafting, filing and prosecution of your cases. Such a document may provide guidance on the drafting of a priority application – with specifics on the specification and the claims, information on fundamental claims, apparatus claims and so forth, and it may include guidance on US provisional applications as first filed applications. There may be useful instructions for using when filing an application claiming priority and it may also cover country or regional specific issues, such as 'means plus function' claims in the US.

However, it is most important that you do not advocate adherence to the guidelines so strongly that the advice, knowledge and insight of the patent agent or attorney is ignored. Ideally, the quality guidelines should be created as a result of an in-depth discussion between all those involved in the patenting process.

Building a strong three-way relationship between the inventor, the person within your Patent Creation Factory handling the case, and the person in the External Patent Agency company handling the case may be needed, particularly with a complex case.

Conflict of interest is an important issue when outsourcing work to an External Patent Agency, because it is almost certain that you are not its only customer. In most countries, External Patent Agencies have ethical rules to follow on how to manage and hopefully avoid such conflicts.

Regular auditing of your External Patent Agencies is something that should form part of your management programme. Respectful but direct feedback to an External Patent Agency on non-performance is important and this example should be set very early in the relationship. If your agents are not meeting commitments, you must call on them immediately, because this sets the rules and expectations immediately. It is also helpful to ask others how an External Patent Agency is performing, because although the interface to you may be great, there may be problems in other parts of the business, such as accounting. There are several ways of auditing your External Patent Agencies and you may wish to perform or coordinate an audit with the support of other departments, such as Finance, IT and/or Security. A full audit means evaluating the External Patent Agency against your supplier requirements and this audit should be formal and done under a qualified lead auditor. This audit assessment may be initiated by asking the External Patent Agency to complete a self-assessment questionnaire, which is then backed-up by an onsite visit.

Gathering feedback from the External Patent Agencies and reacting to any valid concerns they may have on your performance is another key part of this management programme. It is important to listen to your External Patent Agencies and understand what they are looking for out of the business relationship. They are almost certainly looking for commitment and a degree of trust and they will not appreciate being beaten up for pennies or threatened with loss of business. There should also be follow through on any verbal discussions, fact based performance feedback and an infrequent bid process. Payment issues should be dealt with swiftly (there are always payment issues) and you should take a judicious approach to problem resolution.

Here is a simple checklist of issues to consider when managing your External Patent Agencies:

- formal agreements;

- pricing models;

- quality guidelines;

- global list of your approved External Patent Agencies created, maintained and shared;

- good understanding of their skills and competencies;

- information sharing with the External Patent Agencies;

- task management and allocation process defined and agreed;

- three-way relationships in place for at least complex cases;

- conflict of interest defined, and issues discussed and resolved;

- regular audits;

- feedback mechanism in place.

# What is expected from you?

The responsibility for ensuring a good professional working relationship with an External Patent Agency does not rest alone with the External Patent Agency. There are also responsibilities for you, the customer in the relationship.

These responsibilities include management and development of the relationship and if your relationship is likely to be big volume it is recommended that you nominate a relationship manager. Part of his/her job will include sharing information, if applicable, on strategic plans, roadmaps and other similar developments and also keeping the subcontractor informed of generic company developments and mergers and acquisitions. There needs to be an understanding of the roles and responsibilities of both parties and passing this understanding on to the subcontractor. Customer-specific materials and tools need to be provided to the subcontractor, when needed, and appropriate business contacts should be nominated for individual cases. The relationship manager also needs to ensure the invoicing system and payment process is working efficiently. Outside influences include adherence to relevant laws, regulations and ethical guidelines or similar.

> *"One of the things I learned when I was negotiating was that until I changed myself, I could not change others."* Nelson Mandela

# Associations for External Patent Agencies

There are External Patent Agency societies, associations and bodies in place, which have been set up to regulate the conduct of their members. In the UK, there is the Chartered Institute of Patent Attorneys (CIPA) and this is the professional and examining body for patent attorneys (also known as patent agents) in the UK. The institute has issued rules of professional conduct for all its members. In the USA, there is AIPLA, the American Intellectual Property Law Association. There is also an association in China called the All China Patent Agents Association (ACPAA).

The purpose of these associations is generally the same:

- maintain a register of patent attorneys or agents on behalf of the respective governments;

- advise the government and other bodies on patent policy and practice matters;

- maintain a code of conduct for members to observe;

- provide training for members;

- organise patent workshops for members of the public;

- provide information to the general public.

All members who join such societies, associations or bodies must agree to abide by their 'rules of professional conduct'. These are written to ensure that clients receive accurate and impartial advice that puts the interests of the client foremost. As an example, Figure 9.1 shows CIPA's rules of conduct.

**Chartered Institute of Patent Attorneys (CIPA) rules of professional conduct:**

All members who join the Institute agree to abide by the Institute's Rules of Professional Conduct. These are written to ensure that clients consulting a firm of patent attorneys receive accurate and impartial advice that puts their interests foremost.

General

1. A Member shall practice competently, conscientiously and objectively, putting clients' interests foremost and respecting clients' confidence while observing the law and the Member's duty to Any Court or Tribunal.

2. A Member's conduct shall be such as to promote well-founded public confidence in the intellectual property system, in the Institute and in its Members.

Availability

3. When unwilling to provide services, or withdrawing them, a Member shall make reasonable effort in the circumstances to enable the person wishing to use those services to make other arrangements.

Conflicts of Interest

4. Except with the approval of the clients concerned, a Member shall not act for a client on any particular matter if, having acted for another client on a conflicting matter, the Member's professional duty to either client may thereby be compromised.

5. A Member shall not act for a client if, without the knowledge and approval of that client, the member has, or acquires, any significant interest that the Member knows, or could reasonably be expected to know, may conflict with the Member's professional duty to that client.

Source: http://www.cipa.org.uk/download_files/rules.pdf

The Chartered Institute of Patent Attorneys (CIPA) is the professional and examining body for patent attorneys (also known as patent agents) in the UK.

The Institute was founded in 1882 and was incorporated by Royal Charter in 1891. It represents virtually all the 1,500 registered patent attorneys in the UK whether they practice in industry or in private practice.

**Figure 9.1** Chartered Institute of Patent Attorneys (CIPA) rules of professional conduct.

# Outsourcing the management of the payment of annuity fees

Once the patent has been granted, there are still annuity fees to be paid in order to keep the patent alive and you must weigh up whether the decision to use an external company for the management and payment of such fees makes sense for your company. The handling of annuity fees is very much a core business activity for certain companies and it may not make sense to allocate your limited resources to this type of activity.

# What can go wrong?

Generally things can go wrong with any external suppliers when you yourself do not know what you actually want to purchase. You must be clear on what you expect of your External Patent Agency, what the work results should be and how it should communicate with you, because just setting up agreements and a pricing structure is not enough. You will need to monitor that the agreed rates are adhered to and appear on invoices and that the supplier complies with the agreement. Lastly, in the case of fault or non-performance you must utilise the remedies and sanctions provided in the agreement.

External Patent Agency management and relation- ship management should be carried out in a professional manner and the people dealing with External Patent Agencies should have adequate competency and information on how the External Patent Agencies are to be managed.

# Summary

The decision on whether to allocate tasks internally or externally is a difficult one. There is no 'right' way and the appropriate decision varies between companies and situations, because there are many factors to take into consideration. This can be compared to a pendulum swinging from internal to external and back again and never quite remaining at either end.

Almost every single activity within the Patent Creation Factory can be treated as a commodity, meaning that you can obtain quotations for any activity you are intending to outsource.

Whatever conclusion is reached, External Patent Agencies will be needed at some point as not everything can be done in-house, due to different legal requirements in different countries.

When you make the decision to outsource one or more of your activities, your selection of External Patent Agencies to carry out this work should ultimately be based on the service practice of that vendor and the people assigned to actually carry out the work.

No two External Patent Agency firms are the same. Larger firms tend to have more competencies and the capacity to deal with fluctuating needs and they also are more used to developing their business and personnel independent from any one customer. The bigger firms are able to maintain a larger customer base and they are not so dependent on your work alone, making them healthier from a business perspective. The smaller External Patent Agencies may however be more flexible and agile in responding to your needs and even willing to change their own processes to suit yours. Larger firms can more easily arrange customer specific teams to work around conflict issues, whereas smaller firms may need to reject work from some other customers if they wish to work with you.

The management of External Patent Agencies is, in many ways, very similar to the management of in-house resource; it's all about fact-based management and values-based leadership.

# 10
# Metrics

## Introduction

This chapter focuses on the essential metrics that a business must consider and assess in order to monitor and measure the performance of their Patent Creation Factory. It provides information on why metrics are important and what needs to be measured and calculated within any Patent Creation Factory.

Traditional factories are very at ease using metrics and it is not uncommon to have the walls of a factory decorated with various metrics charts, informing the employees within the factory about pass rates, quality, production and process times.

Metrics enable calculations and comparisons to be made of the factory in order to establish whether it is running effectively and efficiently and in line with targets. This chapter introduces you to the subject and guides you through the process of selecting and developing a metrics system that best suits your Patent Creation Factory.

It is important to note that you generally get what you measure, therefore it is essential to decide upon the correct measure. There are indeed plenty of examples of failures due to the incorrect metrics being monitored, or rather, the failure to monitor and measure the correct metrics.

> *"The more you understand what is wrong with a figure, the more valuable that figure becomes."*
> Sir William Thompson

I discuss and evaluate the various metrics available, highlighting the variable nature of the subject; as each and every Patent Creation Factory will require a different metric system, depending upon its specific circumstances and objectives. This chapter provides you with the information and necessary techniques in order to make an assessment of your Patent Creation Factory with respect to metrics.

# Definition of metrics

Metrics are a set of parameters or ways of quantitative and periodic assessment of a process that is to be measured, along with the procedures on how to conduct such measurement, plus the procedures for interpretation of the results if necessary.

**Table 10.1**  Definition of a metric (reproduced by permission of ISM3)

| Metric | Name of the metric |
|---|---|
| Metric description | Description of what is measured |
| Measurement procedure | How the metric is measured |
| Measurement frequency | How often the measurement is taken |
| Threshold estimations | How are the thresholds calculated |
| Current thresholds | Current range of values considered normal for the metric |
| Target value | Best possible value for the metric |
| Units | Units of measurement |

Table 10.1 suggests the elements that must be known for a metric to be fully defined, although such level of formality may not be required for every element selected for metrics by the Patent Creation Factory.

# Why are metrics important?

Metrics are important because they ultimately act as a means to measure the success of your business. Collectively, they provide a checklist through which you can ensure the maintenance or continuity of a successful practice or a means to highlight the reasons behind a specific failure, and consequently permit one to alter a practice in order to improve performance.

Each metric possesses its own justification as to why it is important and this will depend on what it intends to measure.

Certain metrics prove particularly useful to the senior management of a company because they highlight the effectiveness or efficiency of a practice, and often the result of the measure has a direct impact on how senior management respond. This indicates that there should be an alignment between the metric, the result and the response. With the ever-increasing importance of intellectual property rights (IPR), it is only natural that senior company managers are paying more attention to their IPR function, and with this in mind metrics are more frequently being applied in order to measure the success of organisations. A competent system of metrics is a prerequisite to the successful management and leadership of any Patent Creation Factory, without which businesses would struggle to measure and monitor their effectiveness and efficiency.

Furthermore, metrics can aid in spotting general trends in a particular industry. Whether they are successful or unsuccessful trends, metrics highlight certain practices, which share certain aspects that companies should either emulate or avoid depending on their respective success. Metrics therefore act as a valuable tool in ensuring progress within industries and reducing the risk of failure.

Certain metrics are longer in nature than others. Some may only possess a short-term goal whereas others envisage a longer duration. The latter will require a greater degree of monitoring and perhaps a greater allocation of resources. On the other hand, a short-term metric may be less reliable as it only focuses on a short period of time. Although some metrics may be better suited to a longer time frame, this is not always necessary.

Finally, some metrics are more important than others, although this will ultimately depend on the priorities of the person measuring a practice. For example, a professional with a financial background is more likely to attribute greater significance to the cost of a product, while someone with an artistic background may place more weight on the quality of the product.

> *"To measure is to know."*   Sir William Thompson

# Elements that can be measured

In the world of intellectual property and especially within the Patent Creation Factory, many elements can be measured.

Time and energy will need to be spent on evaluating the various elements and deciding on the measures you really want to monitor. The correct metrics to select depend to a degree on your own situation, so there are no right or wrong answers as such and it is up to you to decide which measures will produce the best gains for your company.

There are a small number of critical metrics related to the management and leadership of the Patent Creation Factory and these focus on issues such as quality, costs, effectiveness and efficiency. Quality and costs will be studied in greater detail in Chapters 11 and 12.

A large number of potential metrics are related to steps in the core process, focusing on how well each phase in the core

**Table 10.2** Example of some measurable elements

| | IRs Received | IRS Received (Cumulative) | IRs Handled | IRs Handled (Cumulative) | Accepted | Accepted (Cumulative) | First Filing | First Filing (Cumulative) | % Acceptance Rate |
|---|---|---|---|---|---|---|---|---|---|
| | | | | *Invention Report and First Filing Data* | | | | | |
| January | 48 | 48 | 31 | 31 | 8 | 8 | 6 | 6 | 25.81% |
| February | 36 | 84 | 34 | 65 | 8 | 16 | 6 | 12 | 23.53% |
| March | 43 | 127 | 44 | 109 | 11 | 27 | 8 | 20 | 25.00% |
| April | 34 | 161 | 35 | 144 | 7 | 34 | 10 | 30 | 20.00% |
| May | 38 | 199 | 37 | 181 | 10 | 44 | 10 | 40 | 27.03% |

process is working and helping to identify any bottlenecks or problem areas.

There are metrics related to customer satisfaction, which relate to how well the Patent Creation Factory is performing in the management of its key interfaces to the inventor community and the other parts of IPR. This also includes a company's senior management, business and technology units, and the External Patent Agencies and other IPR organisations.

Some metrics are related to the personnel within the Patent Creation Factory, such as employee satisfaction levels, staff turnover, formal qualifications obtained and job rotations.

Finally, there are a number of external metrics worth considering, such as published league tables.

## Specific metrics

Any Patent Creation Factory will have a number of different areas in which metrics can be used to help measure their own relative successes. This book has looked at a number of different aspects ranging from the core activities of a Patent Creation Factory, to factors that should be considered in order to help improve its performance. Each of these areas can be broken down and in doing so one can highlight a number of key metrics that are essential to measure in any business.

To start with you may wish to consider a number of metrics that can be used in assessing the basic raw material of your

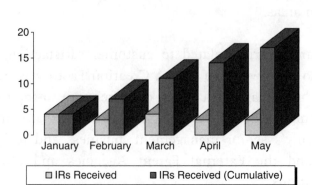

**Figure 10.1** Metrics showing the number of invention Reports received by technological area.

factory: your ideas. These metrics may range from the number of inventions recorded (Figure 10.1), the number of inventions in your core areas of interest or the number of inventions outside your core area interest. Alternatively, you may wish to calculate the acceptance rate for your recorded inventions or the time it takes from the recording of an invention report to its review or to first filing.

When assessing your factory's core activities you may want to consider metrics that are related to your filing and prosecution activities and therefore to review the number of first filings that your company achieves (Figure 10.2) or the number of patent applications that progress to a granted patent.

You can assess your inventor community by measuring the total number of inventors in relation to your total employee population. Using this ratio acts as a guide to the innovative level of your business. Alternatively, you may prefer to calcu-

First Filings by Classification

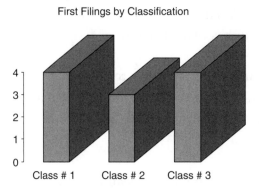

**Figure 10.2** Metrics showing the number of first filings by classification.

Acceptance Rate %

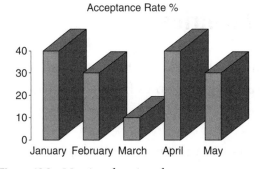

**Figure 10.3** Metrics showing the acceptance rate.

late your acceptance rate (Figure 10.3), the percentage of serial inventors within your inventor community, the percentage of properly completed invention reports or even the percentage of invention reports pushed by inventors, in comparison to the amount pulled by IPR.

Customer satisfaction is essential to any business, so it is imperative that any business has measures in place to portray the customer's response accurately. This can be done at several levels including from within a company. Levels of satisfaction from management, the inventor community, IPR and External Patent Agencies all act as an accurate means to assess the success of your factory.

Finally, a business may wish to consider metrics related to workload, ranging from the total workload within patent creation to that spread among the Patent Creation Factory personnel.

Other metrics relating to costs and quality will be considered in greater detail in the following two chapters.

## External metrics

They may not be metrics in the true sense of the word, but there are a number of sources from which it is possible to get external patent data:

- data reports from the patent offices;

- patent league tables or score card reports;

- IP related reports from reputable business analysts;

- IP data direct from individual companies.

Patent offices issue regular, detailed reports. In 2007, the World Intellectual Property Office (WIPO) published a report that highlighted the increased number of patents being granted worldwide. The report used statistics to demonstrate an increase in the level of 'inventiveness and innovation' particularly amongst newly industrialised and emerging countries. This report was comprehensive and incorporated an analysis of patenting activity by field of technology alongside improved statistical data on patent processing and patent life cycles.

Patent 'league tables' and scorecard reports are created by a number of companies. The Patent Board™ cultivates the most accurate patent and patent portfolio database, which includes weekly updates of all patent grants and application data from the United States Patent and Trade Office (USPTO) and the European Patent Office (EPO). The Patent Board™ has a 40-year history analysing patent development and measuring innovation utilising its patent indicators. Each indicator provides an insight into the quality and value of a patent portfolio based on how others have referenced it, how strongly the portfolio is linked to core science and the age of the patent technology that is being built upon. With an accurate measure of your corporate innovation you can make informed strategic decisions such as: Will my patents protect my future revenue stream? Is there an innovative company in the marketplace with whom we should be partnering?

The Patent Board™ publishes the following scorecards: The Global Patent Scorecard™ (GPS), The Patent Board 500™ Scorecard, 17 individual Industry Scorecards™ and The Wall Street Journal's® The Patent Board Scorecard™. The scorecards rank companies based on Technology Strength™ and Science Strength™, which blend patent counts with quality indicators.

The GPS provides unique insight into national technological performance, including strengths in certain technical areas, the impact of patents on the rest of world, the linkage of national innovation with scientific research, and the speed of innovation. It reviews patents issued to the inventors from 59 countries between 1980 and 2007 and can be used as a tool to compare the performance of these countries. The GPS data utilises three distributions of patents; analysed data is classified by i) the US Standard Industrial Classification Product Field (SIC), ii) the International Patent Class (IPC), and iii) The Patent Board's own proprietary set of 30 technology areas.

The Patent Board Scorecard 500™ provides complete indicator data for the Top 500 companies ranked on a normalised Technology Strength™. Normalisation of this ranking indicator allows for cross industry comparisons, factoring out industry dynamics and levelling the playing field. This can help identify highly innovative companies regardless of the industry to which they belong. For companies spanning multiple industries, the calculation is based on a weighted normalisation, factoring in their industry strength based upon their patent activity level within that industry.

Comparing companies' patent portfolios requires an accurate depiction of the patent holdings that a company owns. The Patent Board utilises their proprietary Corporate Ownership Tree™ that involves name normalisation, company unification and adjustments for all restatement, merger and acquisition activity of over 2000 companies, public and private, foreign and domestic.

The individual Industry Scorecards™ look at the patents associated within a single industry. Since many companies have patent holdings across multiple industry sectors, you can get a clear view and a true perspective of competitors' activity. This scorecard helps uncover spikes in technology development and can help you make informed corporate investment decisions. These industry-by-industry rankings are compiled annually. The Patent Scorecard™ has been published in *Business Week*, the *MIT Technology Review*, and is referenced in articles in such publications as the *Chicago Tribune* and *International Herald Tribune*.

In 2007, the *Wall Street Journal* partnered with The Patent Board™ for a weekly feature of the Patent Board Scorecard™ that ranks patent portfolios. The Patent Board™ tracks the patent portfolios of every major patenting firm in the world. The Patent Scorecard™ is a rating of corporate innovation across 17 industries and combines a series of industry-standard metrics to arrive at patent portfolio quality, technological strength and breadth of impact. The Patent Scorecard™ featured in the *Wall Street Journal* is a snapshot measure of the patenting activity averaged over the prior 13-week period focusing on a rotating set of industries each week including automotive, semiconductors, information technology, aerospace and defence, and pharmaceuticals. The Patent Board™ is also featured in bi-monthly articles in the *Intellectual Assets Management* magazine and its weekly blog. The scorecards can help you understand your relative patent portfolio value so you can leverage and protect it. The data and metrics make a connection between past innovation and future success. With patent activity increasing 15 % per year, most companies have significant asset value in patents.

The Institution of Engineering & Technology (IEE) also publishes a patent score card or league table. Their 'Pipeline Power Index' league table takes into account US patents granted for the year, the growth of a company's US patent portfolio, citations, the variety of technologies that build upon a company's patents and the variety of technologies upon which an organisation's patents build.

There are various IP related reports available from reputable business analysts and economic publications, often including IP facts and figures. More and more companies are communicating about their IPR situation and include some facts and figures in their reports. They may not yet include useful data as far as the effectiveness and efficiency of their Patent Creation Factory is concerned, but this may not remain the case forever.

# Setting metrics for others

Defining and agreeing metrics should not be limited to within the Patent Creation Factory, as there is value in setting and agreeing metrics with those groups that will be your key interfaces. There is also value in setting filing targets for those involved in leading product and technology projects within the research and development activities in your organisation, or those involved in large cooperation and collaboration projects with external third parties.

Target setting may sound easy in theory but is often very difficult in practice, especially when setting targets for individuals, teams and groups who are outside the Patent Creation Factory and not under your direct control. In some instances people may wish to look at previous performance figures and then suggest targets that look a 'bit better'. Others may calculate targets as mathematical steps, making fixed increases without any real thought as to how it will be achieved. The setting and monitoring of patent targets is an integral part of the working relationship between the Patent Creation Factory and many of the other groups discussed previously, but you must remember that targets are just one means of managing performance. They can be extremely helpful and powerful, but they are not always appropriate. Blindly setting a target for every activity of value to your factory, for those external individuals, teams and groups outside of your Patent Creation Factory, is unlikely to be productive.

# Summary

Collecting the right information and applying it quickly to improve performance is the true value of any metric, no matter to what part of the Patent Creation Factory it is applied. Make sure that the metrics being used to measure the quality and quantity of your work provide an accurate reflection of how you and your team are doing.

A balance needs to be struck between, on the one hand, establishing and monitoring the metrics for a sufficiently long enough period of time in order to gather useful historical data and, on the other hand, not becoming a slave to the metrics. You should never be afraid to change them when it is needed. Relying too much on metrics can lull you into a false sense of security that everything is fine. It is important to review your selected metrics from time to time to determine if any changes are required in what is being measured and recorded. Certain measures may not change much from week to week or month to month but may have changed more dramatically when reviewed over a longer term.

People become aware of what is being measured and more importantly what is not being measured, so you must be aware that metrics can influence behaviour. Sometimes, selecting the right measures can prompt the right behaviour.

There is a danger that your metrics may focus attention on the overall factory performance or on averages and this may result in you forgetting that each and every patent case is unique.

It is important to understand and appreciate who will be reading and examining the metric reports produced by your Patent Creation Factory. Different readers of the information will typically be interested in different aspects of the metric reports and may focus on certain metrics more than others. IPR Management will be interested in output from the Patent Creation Factory and its overall effectiveness and efficiency, whereas financial experts may focus on associated costs, while technology experts may be interested in the innovation and creativity of the ideas flowing into the Patent Creation Factory.

Although your metrics may not be perfect, conducting a series of measurements following the same methodology, which produce evenly flawed results, may nevertheless prove the trend and may be valuable as such. This is important because hard measures are sometimes difficult to come by for soft targets such as quality. The absence of metrics on soft targets may flaw the overall measuring system towards only hard numbers, thereby favouring the hard numbers (like filing rates) at the cost of quality.

# 11
# Quality

## Introduction

This chapter delves into how a Patent Creation Factory can
ensure the quality of the patents it produces, as well as the
related patent creation processes and activities. The chapter
aims to introduce and demonstrate the important role that
quality and quality assessment plays in such a factory. Challenges that exist in achieving quality and implementing
quality checks are discussed, with the focus on the unique
nature of patents and thus the difficulty of implementing
general quality checks. However, there are ways and means
to overcome such challenges. I will now focus on the various
quality checks that can be deployed and how to implement
them, as well as the related issues and the techniques used
to overcome those issues.

> *"Quality is never an accident; it is always the result of high intention, sincere effort, intelligent direction and skilful execution; it represents the wise choice of many alternatives."*   William A. Foster

# Definition of quality

Quality is about meeting and exceeding expectations. The quality of your patents depends on the quality of the processes you have in place, which in turn is tied to the quality of the management structure of your factory. Quality must be seen as an integral part of patent creation leadership and management. It should be embedded in your strategies, daily decisions and actions, making it everybody's responsibility.

> *"Quality means doing it right when no-one is looking."*   Henry Ford

Quality activities are various and happen at all levels of a Patent Creation Factory. Quality should be defined based on your business needs and common methods and tools, measures and feedback processes needed to continuously monitor and improve performance. The term quality implies a degree of excellence and the quality of a good or service depends upon the criteria being applied to it, so to apply and define a criteria, the expectation level must be set (Figure 11.1).

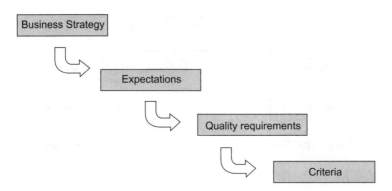

**Figure 11.1** Quality links to business needs.

As in any factory, you should only carry out and monitor the activities that enable you to reach your desired quality level and any measures you decide to put in place should add value and fulfil your business needs.

# Patent quality

Quality relates to patent creation in two ways: first, the quality of your end product, or in other words the patent; and second, the quality of the process in place and of the organisation itself. These two issues must be considered separately because you can have a good quality organisation yet still produce poor quality patents (and vice versa). Therefore the issue of quality is important and must be ensured across the whole spectrum of patent creation (Figure 11.2).

There are some challenges linking quality and patents together and the timescale of the patenting process may be one of the issues. You will be embarking on a long process

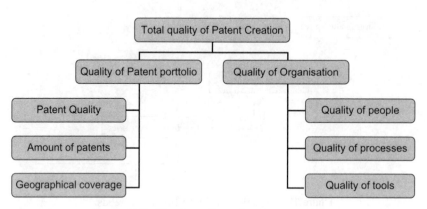

**Figure 11.2** Total quality of patent creation.

when you set out to create a patent and when it is granted you may not need to enforce it for a long period. Subsequently, it may be difficult to determine the quality of your patent because you lack an immediate feedback mechanism. The traditional ways of testing processes do not exist in the world of the Patent Creation Factory as each patent is different and they are not mass-produced. As there is no one single defined measure of patent quality, the following sections identify different ways and means to assess and view quality.

Typically when people think about patent quality they are referring to the quality of the invention and not actually the quality of the patent itself. However, patent quality can and should be considered by looking at the quality of the actual invention and then the quality of the patent protecting the invention (Figure 11.3).

Invention quality can be divided into the quality of the invention itself and the quality of describing the invention. In the case of the invention itself, you have to ask how good your

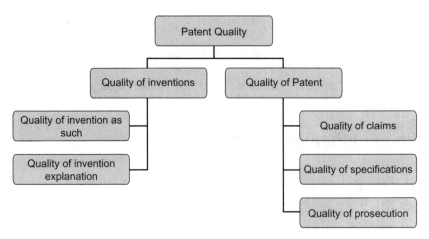

**Figure 11.3**  Patent quality.

original idea is and this may have a direct relationship with the organisation and mode of operation of your Patent Creation Factory and its relationship with the inventor community. A good mode of operation here may entail organising invention hunting camps, conducting brainstorm sessions, or other means that allow you to search for really good ideas. When assessing the quality of the way in which the invention is described, you are essentially asking how well the inventor has communicated the idea and how well the Patent Creation Factory understood it.

# The quality debate in the patent world

There are a number of interesting discussions and developments taking place at the present time in the area of patent quality:

- patent office quality initiatives;

- company led patent quality initiatives;

- research studies into the issue of patent quality.

## Patent office quality initiatives

The US Patent and Trademark Office (USPTO) 2007 year-end results demonstrated a trend of improving patent quality. It released record-breaking year-end numbers that reveal historic improvement in the quality of patent reviews and subsequently the quality of issued patents. The quality numbers are part of the agency's 2007 Performance and Accountability Report.

> *"The sustained trend of quality improvements are a tribute to the internal quality initiatives of our managers and employees. Of course, the quality of patent and trademark examination is a shared responsibility that begins with the application."* Jon Dudas, USPTO Director

In 2007, USPTO's patent examiners examined 362 227 applications, the highest number in the history of the USPTO. Quality compliance was 96.5 %, equalling the 2006 results, the best in 25 years. Patent examiner decisions were upheld by the USPTO's patent appeals board 69 % of the time, up from 51 % 2005.

> *"The USPTO will work tirelessly to ensure high quality agency actions, but we must make progress to ensure examiners are presented with applications that clearly depict the claimed invention and relevant prior art is presented to the examiner in a timely manner."*
> Jon Dudas, USPTO Director

Consistent with Director Dudas' direction, to encourage focused and complete information that allows examiners to make the best decisions when examining applications, the USPTO has initiated a number of improvements to better focus the examination process. These include:

- **Accelerated Examination:** available since August 2006, Accelerated Examination provides applicants with a final determination on their patent application within 12 months. Applicants provide focused and detailed information about their inventions, an explanation as to why their inventions are patentable over the prior art, and the most relevant prior art upon filing their application. Applicants are encouraged to engage in live interviews with the patent examiner.

- **Peer Review:** begun in June 2007 as a joint initiative with the New York Law School's Institute for Information and Policy, the Peer Review is a pilot project that allows technical experts in computer technology the opportunity, for the first time, to submit annotated technical references relevant to the claims of a published patent application before an examiner reviews it. Studies have shown that when patent examiners have the best data in front of them, they make the correct decisions. However, examiners have a limited amount of time to find and properly consider the most relevant information. This is particularly true in the software-related technologies where code is not easily accessible and is often not dated or well-documented.

Of particular note is the relationship among USPTO's quality initiatives, fewer granted patents and higher affirmation rates on appeal. In 2000, a record high of 72 % of all patent applications became patents. In contrast, 51 % of patent applications were granted in 2007. The allowance rate is a function of many aspects, including the quality of the applications received. The USPTO's focus on internal quality control is primarily responsible for the lowered grant rate over the past several years. Looking forward, the USPTO expects that its various applicant-centred initiatives to focus examination will result in clearer applications and thus an increased grant rate, while maintaining a high affirmation rate from the patent appeals board.

## Company led patent quality initiatives

For a number of years now, IBM has had the most number of patents awarded by the USPTO. However, as well as its leadership in the patent volume league table, IBM is also active in the area of patent quality.

IBM is involved in multi-party efforts to increase the review of patent applications, in part by tapping open-source developers and collaborative software. Although the contents of patent applications are public record and available to anyone, IBM has worked with the USPTO to develop the Peer Review already mentioned above. The Peer Review, Peer to Patent, Open Patent Review or Community Patent Review pilot programme allows people, including academics and corporate technologists, to view the content of filed patents easily and provide feedback to patent examiners.

With inventor consent, 250 software related patents will be submitted for open patent examination. The open review supplements, rather than replaces, substantive examination by a USPTO examiner. The process will augment the current rules that permit third party submission of comments for a fee and in writing. For the first time, third parties will be able to submit prior art with commentary online and to encourage participation, the USPTO has waived the fee for third party submissions. The USPTO has offered the further incentive of jumping consenting applications to the front of the queue for expedited review. The pilot has one goal: to ensure that the knowledgeable public can submit prior art relevant to the patent application's claims to the USPTO for consideration.

In another effort, the Open Source Development Labs are hosting a web site called the Open Source Software as Prior Art project (OSAPA), which is designed as a way to search through existing open-source code. IBM, Novell, Red Hat and OSTG (SourceForge.net) are participating in the project and the goal is to reduce the number of poor quality patents that issue by increasing accessibility to Open Source Software code and documentation that can be used as prior art during the patent examination process. OSAPA originated back in December 2005 when the USPTO met with members of the Open Source community and industry to discuss ways in which they could collaborate to improve the quality of patents, including software patents.

> *"Collaboration between the Patent Office and the open-source community builds on the momentum of the open-source model. There is powerful logic in tapping vast public resources to address the growing public interest in patent quality."* John Doll, Commissioner for Patents at the Patent Office

The third initiative, the Patent Quality Index (PQI), calls for a system to rank the quality of the patent application. IBM is supporting the work of Professor Ronald Mann at Columbia Law School, who is now directing this effort. The current plan for the PQI focuses on analysing the characteristics of the small number of patents for which there is definitive information about validity available, patents on which the Federal Circuit Court in the USA has issued a decision that the patent is invalid or not invalid. The PQI project has collected a dataset of the 235 most recently litigated patents from the Federal Circuit, as well as a matched set of patents that were not litigated. Preliminary analysis of seven data points (claims, forward references, total references, domestic references, foreign references, non-patent prior art, and pages) suggests that the valid patents differ from their matches in a much more positive way than the invalid patents. This is intriguing for two reasons. First, it suggests that there is an objective foundation to the validity decisions of the Federal Circuit. Second, it holds open the promise of identifying objective characteristics of patents and applications that relate with sufficient reliability to the ultimate holding of validity, so that they can be used to establish filters or hurdles in the patent prosecution process. In the next stage of the project, the PQI project plans to collect several dozen additional data points from the prosecution histories, extending their analysis to identify the characteristics that most reliably relate to the quality of the issued patent.

## Research and study into the issue of patent quality

The Intellectual Property Owners Association (IPO), established in 1972, is a trade association for owners of patents, trademarks, copyrights and trade secrets. The IPO conducted a survey in 2005 (available at http://www.ipo.org/ PatentQualityReport) to measure perceptions of its members, concerning the quality of patents issued in the US. The questionnaire was sent to 139 companies, all of which were IPO corporate members and patent holders. Just over half of the respondents (51.3 %) rated the quality of patents issued in the US today as less than satisfactory or poor (47.5 % less than satisfactory and 3.8 % poor). A smaller percentage of 8.8 % of respondents rated the patent quality as more than satisfactory or outstanding (8.8 % more than satisfactory and 0 % outstanding). The final 40 % of the respondents rated the quality of patents as satisfactory. The detailed survey results provided data broken down by industry type and by company annual revenue.

> *"IPO believes that higher patent quality is critically important for boosting American technology and reducing business litigation."*     IPO President J. Jeffrey Hawley

New research has shown that patent applications in emerging technologies are judged inconsistently.

New research by Assistant Professor of Strategic and International Management at London Business School, Markus Reitzig, and his co-author Paul Burke (University of Technology, Sydney) aims to investigate the ongoing discussion about decreasing 'patent quality', which is often linked to decreasing patent office 'service quality' by the popular press, policy makers, and academics.

The authors argue that patent quality can be defined along two major dimensions: the techno-(economic) quality created by the patent's underlying invention, and the legal quality created by the patent's reliability as an enforceable property right. The patent office's role in providing a worthwhile service is therefore twofold. First, it must consistently assess the initial patent application and grant patents only to those applications that meet patentability criteria. Second, it must enforce consistent judgment upon challenged patents. The quality of these assessments has been heavily debated – especially in emerging areas like software and nanotechnology.

Reitzig and his colleague put up two central questions for a test: how consistently did the European Patent Office (EPO) base patent decisions on its judgments of past technological quality? What were the sources of inconsistent judgments between patent grant and challenge?

Using data on European biotechnology patents filed between 1978 and 1987 the authors showed that the EPO's decision-making on a patent's technological quality during the granting phase and during the opposition phase – where the granting of the patent is legally challenged by third parties – was not consistent as far as can be told from bibliographic indicators. Moreover, the researchers found no compelling indications that the inconsistency was due to the fact that more information was available, and more resources allocated, towards judging the patent's technological quality at the end of the opposition procedure. Thus at least in the area surveyed, examiners and opposition divisions judge seemingly identical information in different ways, something that is clearly undesirable.

'It appears as if the uncertainty associated with patent protection in emerging technological areas is high and it appears very difficult to predict whether, in such industries, a patent – once granted – will be sustained during legal challenges in the future,' Reitzig says. 'Without blaming anyone, this may simply be due to the inherent difficulty of the task of evaluating the patentability of technologies from novel technological areas.'

However, this also impacts on how managers judge these new ventures. On top of the technological and market uncertainty that characterises ventures in these areas, the legal uncertainty needs to be factored in. 'Currently, we tend to think that once patent protection status is reached we're safe. This may not necessarily be the case,' Reitzig and Burke argue.

The article describing the research appears in *Research Policy*, 2007, **36**(9), 1404–1430.

# Quality guidelines

Another approach to help ensure consistency across your patent portfolio is to create a requirements specification document or a quality guidelines document, for use by all patent agents or attorneys drafting, filing and prosecuting cases on your behalf. Quality guidelines, rather than a requirements specification, is a more apt term because it may not be possible or desirable to specify everything to the nth degree, as some flexibility may be required. The goal of such guidelines is to provide some level of consistency in the drafting, filing and prosecuting of your cases.

Such a document may provide, for example, guidance on the drafting of a priority application, with specifics on the specification and the claims. It may provide information on fundamental claims, apparatus claims and so forth and it may include guidance on US Provisional applications as first filed applications. It may contain useful instructions when filing an application claiming priority. It may also cover country or regional specific issues such as 'means plus function' claims in the US.

However, it is most important not to push the guidelines so strongly that the advice, knowledge and insight of the patent agent or attorney is ignored. Ideally, the quality guidelines should be created as a result of an in-depth discussion between all those involved in the patenting process.

By issuing these guidelines, you are attempting to improve the quality of your patent applications while still complying with the laws and rules of the pertinent jurisdiction. If your patent agent or attorney believes that an approach that is suggested or mandated in these guidelines violates a law or regulation in a given country, he or she should bring the matter to your attention at the earliest convenience. Furthermore, if he or she believes that there is a better way to achieve your objectives than the approaches set forth in your guidelines, again this should be brought to your attention. The contents of your quality guidelines are not meant to be set in stone and will need updating and improving from time to time, based on, among other things, changes in patent law and advice and input from patent experts.

The quality guidelines should stress, however, that if the patent agent or attorney drafting a particular case on your behalf does not have sufficient knowledge of your businesses, your products or services and/or the pertinent industry or technology to comply properly with any of the guidelines you outlined, that patent attorney or agent must seek that knowledge. Indeed, prior to drafting the application or at some point early in the drafting process, the attorney or agent should seek the necessary information from the inventors and/or an appropriate person within the Patent Creation Factory.

## Organisation quality

People are critical because the patenting process cannot be automated. It is, however, possible to measure the quality and professionalism of the people involved in the process, the quality of the tools they are using and the quality of the process itself (Figure 11.4).

Both internal and external measures may be used to measure the quality of people's professional qualifications, reputations, white papers, etc. Before entering this stage, however, you should ask yourself how simple and straightforward the patenting process is and then proceed by checking each phase of it: drafting, filing, reviewing, granting and the level of

**Figure 11.4**  Organisational quality.

objection. Always remember that the quality of the decision-making is a key metric that you should not overlook. Ask what information, such as the original invention, patent analysis and expert opinions, are needed to allow a good decision to be made. You should be able to identify who is involved in decision-making and you must ensure that a balance is struck between the need to make timely decisions and the need to make well informed decisions. Everyone concerned must be informed of this decision. In addition, ask yourself the following questions. How good are the tools you are using and have you compared and contrasted them to tools used by others? Are the tools the best in the industry and are they likely to help or hinder your chances of success?

The idea here is to measure data integrity or measure the quality of the documentation involved. Everything is recorded in the world of the Patent Creation Factory because you must write down the initial idea, the searches you have done, all correspondence, draft documents and any documents submitted. Since everything is written down, you can review the quality of that documentation, in terms of its accuracy and completeness.

# Improving quality

There are several ways and means to establish a quality culture within the Patent Creation Factory and to work around some of the challenges faced. If you wish to improve and maintain quality you need to put some quality systems and checks in place (Figure 11.5).

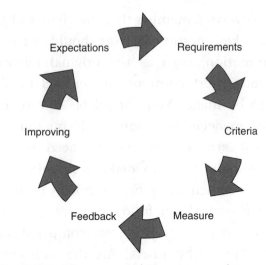

**Figure 11.5** The process of improving quality.

Good quality constructive feedback can be a very useful tool to help improve quality levels. The basic idea is to get those people who actually utilise the patents to provide feedback to those in patent creation although this feedback will of course be limited and based solely on those particular patents selected to be used. The people providing feedback will typically be involved in patent licensing and litigation activities. In many intellectual property organisations, different people are involved in the drafting, filing and prosecution of cases compared to those involved in licensing and litigation. The challenge is that there will be no case specific feedback for at least three to six years, and so it is a very slow mechanism. How well cases perform in licensing and litigation battles provides some indication of the quality of these cases.

As you move forward in your quality initiatives you must ask yourself some fundamental questions. Does a quality culture permeate the factory and how is it measured? Are employees quizzed or surveyed about various issues on a regular basis, and if so, is quality one of the subjects raised?

Building a quality culture throughout the Patent Creation Factory is not an easy task. Developing a focus on quality may seem very easy but it really is not straightforward to achieve and, as usual with any improvements, it will start with a gap analysis. Looking at your factory now from a quality perspective, where is it and what are you hoping to achieve? Although your factory may be very small, there will be some good points to keep or possibly enhance even further.

After finding the gaps, an action plan is needed to address the shortcomings. You will need to develop your own factory wide quality standards and to do this you need to study what suits your factory the best and then apply the right balance. A commitment to total patent quality from senior management is a 'MUST'.

As is true with any successful implementation, you need the right team blend and capable people in the team to execute these quality improvement plans. Capabilities are needed in terms of skill sets and experience because skills alone, without maturity, cannot sustain the quality gains you achieve. People leading and driving quality are required to be skilled and experienced in terms of their understanding of total patent quality. Then and only then can they define the quality improvement plan, bring that plan to execution and ensure that others are following the plan.

There will be a need to raise the basic knowledge, understanding and maturity for each and every member of the Patent Creation Factory. For this purpose factory wide training needs to be arranged and the experienced trainer should impart training that convinces staff that they need to embrace and support the quality initiatives.

> *"Quality is not an act, it is a habit."*   Aristotle

However hard you try to improve quality, it will fail if people are not motivated. Remember that not everyone is self-motivated and senior management and the leaders of your quality improvement initiatives need to provide a sufficient amount of motivation to drive things ahead. However, a certain amount of enforcement is also required to push the changes in the system and you need to ensure there is the correct mix of both. Ultimately your wish is to institutionalise quality within your Patent Creation Factory. Regular quality audits must be conducted, and action taken based on the key findings, and quality reports should also be generated and distributed. All these steps will help to create a quality culture that permeates the entire Patent Creation Factory.

## Summary

In conclusion, this chapter has focused on quality and what it is, how to ensure it and ways to transfer theory into practice. It provides you with the required knowledge to check that the system you have in place is doing what you want it to and working to the required standard. At the same time, take care that you do not spend so much time measuring the process and the data integrity that you lose sight of the quality of the patents granted.

> *"In communities where men build ships for their own sons to fish or fight from, quality is never a problem."*
> J. Deville

# 12

# Patent cost management

## Patent cost management

Patents and the processes involved in patent creation can be expensive and therefore costs must be weighed carefully and managed well. Cost management involves the planning, coordination, control and reporting of all cost related aspects of your Patent Creation Factory. It is the process of identifying all costs associated with the investment, making informed choices about the options that will deliver the best value for money and managing those costs throughout the life of the patent or patents. Decisions about cost must be based on an understanding of the whole supply chain involved in patent creation and must be weighed against the immense value that patents generate for business. Cost management is an essential part of effective and efficient factory management.

The costs that can be incurred vary considerably from country to country, depending on factors such as the nature of the invention, its complexity, attorney's fees, the length of the application and objections raised during the examination by the patent office. Therefore it is extremely important to keep in mind and properly manage the costs related to patent creation.

Despite an increased awareness among businesses of the benefits of using the intellectual property (IP) system, many still fail to manage their IP assets to their full potential. Although the costs of obtaining and maintaining a patent may be significant at first, it should be noted that patent costs are only a small fraction of the total cost incurred in turning an invention into a commercially useful product and of marketing and selling it in the relevant market. If it is clear that the profits arising from the product are not proportionate to the costs involved, you should not patent the invention.

## The patent cost curve

Before I examine patent costs and patent cost management in detail, it is useful to take a top-level look at the patent cost curve.

Estimating patent costs is admittedly a difficult matter because so much depends on the nature of the invention, the technology involved, the geographical coverage selected and whether in-house or external patent attorneys are to handle the case, plus many other factors. What must and should be understood and appreciated is that obtaining a patent can be expensive. Having said this, not all the money required to obtain a patent has to be paid upfront and you will be able

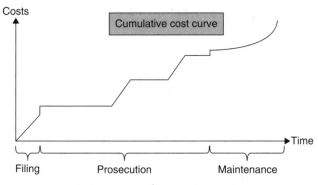

**Figure 12.1**   A typical patenting cost curve.

to stagger the investment over time. However, just as in any endeavour requiring financial resources, a realistic budget will make all the difference. The simple chart in Figure 12.1 illustrates the typical patenting cost curve. Interestingly it shows that patenting costs are spread over a number of years and that the cost curve is not flat but generally increasing over time, although the exact cost curve will vary from patent to patent.

Three key elements contribute to the overall costs of obtaining a patent: the official fees as specified by the relevant patent office(s); the fees charged for the work conducted by the patent attorney handling the case; and your own internal Patent Creation Factory costs. The good news is that most cost information is readily available because patent offices and External Patent Agencies publish their fees, so that you can see in advance what costs you are going to incur if you decide to proceed. The bad news is that the fee structures tend to be somewhat complex, and it can be difficult for the first timer to really understand all the various elements that will contribute to the overall patent cost.

# Official patent office fees

Table 12.1 shows the costs that can be incurred when applying for a patent from the UK Patent Office, although the latest up-to-date official fee cost table is readily available from the Patent Office itself. With this table you can see all the costs you will be expected to pay in the process of an application as well as the cost of annuities to keep your patent alive once it has been granted. Similar cost tables can be found for other national patent offices with their subsequent charges.

Although none of the individual items listed appear to be that expensive, when they are added together, it is a different matter indeed. Of course, not every item listed may apply to you and your particular patent application and it is worth noting that many of the items listed in Table 12.1 refer to work items being late, requests for changes or corrections and requests for extending a particular time limit. It is also worth noting how the renewal fees to maintain the granted patent increase from year to year.

The fees in many patent offices for obtaining patents and then renewing them have increased substantially in recent years, because governments require the patent offices to obtain more of their income from users than the taxpayer. On the other hand, patent offices are trying to help reduce costs in some areas. The London Agreement on the application of Article 65 of the European Patent Convention (EPC) was signed in October 2000, and signatories agreed to waive the requirement for translations of European patents to be filed in their national language. In practice, therefore, applicants do not

**Table 12.1**  UK Patent Office costs

| Action | Cost (£) |
|---|---|
| International patent application – entry to national phase | 30 |
| Publication of translation | 12 |
| Application fee for a patent application | 30 |
| Request for grant of patent | no charge |
| Initiation of proceedings before the Comptroller | 50 |
| Surrender of patent proceeding | no charge |
| Late declaration [rule 6A(2)] | 150 |
| Late claim | 40 |
| Statement of inventorship and of right to grant a patent | no charge |
| Request for certificate authorising the release of a sample of biological material | no charge |
| Notice of the intention to restrict the availability of samples of biological material to experts | no charge |
| Request for a preliminary examination and search in respect of an international application for a patent (UK) that has already been subject to a search by the International Search Authority | 100 |
| Request for a preliminary examination and search in respect of any other application | 130 |
| Request for a further search under section 17(6) or payment for a supplementary search under section 17(8) | 100 |
| Citations | 15 |
| Request for a search under section 17(1) for an international application that has been searched in the international phase | 80 |
| Request for a search under section 17(1) for any other application | 100 |
| Request for a further search under section 17(6) or payment for a supplementary search under section 17(8) | 100 |

**Table 12.1**  Continued

| Action | Cost (£) |
| --- | --- |
| Citations, per extra copy | 15 |
| Request for a substantive examination | 70 |
| Request to make an amendment or correction | 40 |
| Payment of renewal fee (and additional fee for late payment): | |
| Renewal – 5th year | 50 |
| Renewal – 6th year | 70 |
| Renewal – 7th year | 90 |
| Renewal – 8th year | 110 |
| Renewal – 9th year | 130 |
| Renewal – 10th year | 150 |
| Renewal – 11th year | 170 |
| Renewal – 12th year | 190 |
| Renewal – 13th year | 210 |
| Renewal – 14th year | 230 |
| Renewal – 15th year | 250 |
| Renewal – 16th year | 270 |
| Renewal – 17th year | 300 |
| Renewal – 18th year | 330 |
| Renewal – 19th year | 360 |
| Renewal – 20th year | 400 |
| Additional fees for late payment of renewal fee: | |
| Not exceeding one month | no charge |
| Each succeeding month (but not exceeding six months) | 24 |
| Request to reinstate a patent application | 150 |
| Notice of opposition to proceedings before the Comptroller | 50 |

**Table 12.1** Continued

| Action | Cost (£) |
| --- | --- |
| Application to restore a patent | 135 |
| Request for opinion as to validity or infringement | 200 |
| Request to alter a name or address | no charge |
| Application to register or give notice of rights acquired in a patent or in an application for a patent | no charge |
| Request for a certificate of the Comptroller or a certified or uncertified copy from file or the register – sealed | 22 |
| Request for a certificate of the Comptroller or a certified or uncertified copy from file or the register – stamped | 16 |
| Request for a certificate of the Comptroller or a certified or uncertified copy from file or the register – uncertified copies | 5 |
| Application by the proprietor of a patent for an entry to be made in the register that licences under the patent are available as of right | no charge |
| Application by the proprietor of a patent to cancel an entry in the register that licences under the patent are available as of right | no charge |
| Request to be informed of future events relating to a patent application or patent (caveat) | 25 |
| Appointment or change of agent | No charge |
| Request to extend a prescribed time limit | 135 |
| Payment of an additional fee for the restoration of a patent or for a discretionary extension of time or period | 135 |
| Filing a translation in connection with a European patent or a European patent application | no charge |
| Declaration by the proprietor of a patent that licences of right under the patent shall not extend to excepted uses | no charge |
| Renewal payment date information | 5 |

have to translate the specification of their patents for London Agreement contracting countries that have one of the three EPO languages (English, French and German) as an official language or which have prescribed one of those three languages for the purposes of the Agreement. To enter into force, the Agreement must be ratified by eight countries, including the UK, France and Germany and it is estimated that translation costs will be reduced by an average of 45 % once the Agreement comes into effect. Signatory states can still require the translation of patent claims into their national languages.

In an increasing number of countries, governments and other funding agencies that provide grants or subsidies for research and development and innovation activities to research institutes, universities and enterprises have begun to allow a portion of funds to be used for meeting patenting costs. In certain schemes this even extends to covering filing costs. As part of your cost management activities, it would be worthwhile investigating whether such support schemes are available to you.

## Patent attorney fees

Official patent office fees are only one factor to consider when calculating the total cost of patenting. The cost of a patent application and its prosecution costs depend on a number of factors such as:

- nature of the invention;

- core technology involved;

- quality of the invention report created by the inventor;

- length of the patent application documentation;

- number of claims;

- charges (hourly rate or fixed rate) of the patent agent or attorney handling the case;

- other costs incurred by the patent agent or attorney handling your case;

- fees charged by the draftsperson for preparing any drawings needed;

- total time taken by the attorney/agent in preparing and prosecuting the case;

- nature and number of objections raised by the examiner at the patent office;

- number of countries where you plan to apply for a patent;

- route selected for obtaining foreign filings;

- translation costs;

- whether there are any opposition proceedings or appeals.

As you can see from this list, the patent attorney fees will contribute greatly to the overall patent costs. Reputable External Patent Agencies, however, publish the fees they will charge you for handling your case and helping you achieve your goal of 'idea to granted patent'.

Apart from understanding the charges by the External Patent Agency, it is also worth giving consideration on its invoicing practice. There are two basic models in use:

- **Task based billing** – you receive an invoice every time an activity is completed. There are many different forms of task based billed. One invoice may cover sections of work done or you may be invoiced for each specific task.

- **Monthly billing** – you receive an invoice each month for any tasks done within that month. This can be organised on a case basis or task basis.

Every External Patent Agency seems to have its own specific invoicing practice and it is therefore difficult sometimes for a customer to compare the different invoices and this in turn can make it difficult to compare and analyse costs. Sometimes it is advisable to agree on fixed and variable costs. An example of such a cost structure is shown in Table 12.2.

In the example in Table 12.2, when the External Patent Agency is providing services as a foreign filing or local attorney, the same rates are applied. Of course, no drafting work is needed in foreign filing assignments.

The above-specified fixed rates may not include these items that are invoiced at cost against receipts, such as when the customer has accepted expenses in advance in writing, and such as translation expenses, official fees, invoices from foreign associates and drawings made by external suppliers.

Other reimbursements that may be claimed include local and international calls, charges for fax, postage, courier services and photocopies, document preparation, archiving and

**Table 12.2**   An example of a patent agency's invoicing

| | US | Europe | PCT | Other countries/ jurisdictions |
|---|---|---|---|---|
| **Drafting** | Hourly rate | Hourly rate | Hourly rate | Hourly rate |
| **First filing** | Fixed rate | Fixed rate | Fixed rate | Hourly rate |
| **National/ conventional filing** | Fixed rate | Fixed rate | Fixed rate | Fixed rate |
| | Japan/China/Korea: fixed rate | | | |
| **Patent prosecution** | Hourly rate for attorney work | | | |
| • **Technical office action** | Fixed rate for other work as below: | | | |
| **Patent prosecution** | | | | |
| • **Non-technical office action** | Fixed rate | Fixed rate | Fixed rate | Fixed rate |
| • **Information disclosure statements (US only)** | Fixed rate | | | |
| • **Publication** | Fixed rate | Fixed rate | Fixed rate | Fixed rate |
| • **Examination** | Fixed rate | Fixed rate | Fixed rate | Fixed rate |
| • **Grant phase** | Fixed rate | Fixed rate | N/A | Fixed rate |

secretarial overtime. There could also be charges for invoices from overseas associates, the hire of meeting facilities and hospitality; and general travelling expenses including the cost of hotels and evening meals, taxis or car hire.

The management of External Patent Agencies was considered in greater detail in Chapter 9 and although we have used a cost chart as an example above, this is just one criterion that can be used when selecting an External Patent Agency. It is important to look at total costs when comparing these agencies because there may be hidden costs or certain advantages that one cannot assess in the form of a charge sheet or an invoice.

Patenting cost management tends to focus on patent office official fees and charges by External Patent Agencies. However costs are involved in running your Patent Creation Factory, and these cannot be ignored when calculating your total patenting costs. The salaries of your employees, their equipment needs, the office facility and infrastructure, and the various intellectual property specific tools and services they require to do their work must also be included in your planning budget. Training and development of your employees also needs to be considered.

## Keeping track of your patent costs

Perhaps the most obvious ways of managing costs are allocating a sensible budget, having good people to ensure that the budget is well prepared, monitoring actual costs versus planned costs, and then taking appropriate actions when needed. An insufficient budget inevitably results in corners being cut, and the result of this may well mean that the end product is less than satisfactory. On the other hand, too big a budget may cause you to be less than wise in your spending or not to take cost management seriously.

Creating a good patent cost tracking and reporting template is also critical to good cost management. There are many different individual elements to track including the fact that the cost of a patent is spread over such a long period of time, plus the fact that costs are due to three distinct entities: patent office official fees, charges by External Patent Agencies and your own internal Patent Creation Factory costs. Given the complexity of patent costs and the fact that costs can spiral upwards when errors are made or actions are late, plus the fact that the patent cost curve is nonlinear, it is most advisable that you develop and maintain excellent cost tracking and reporting systems.

An example of a patenting cost breakdown structure for tracking and monitoring purposes is shown in Figure 12.2.

Figure 12.2 is just one example of how your business may wish to manage your costs and the template segregates costs into four distinct sections: first filing costs, prosecution costs, foreign filing costs and the cost of annuity payments. These are later split into periodic payments, in this case depending upon the cost being monthly or quarterly. Finally, average costs are then predicted to give an overall impression of how resources should be distributed between each section.

Tools are available to help you estimate your patent costs, and being able to predict the likely costs prior to them arising and allocating your budget accordingly subsequently enables you to distribute resources proportionately. Global IP Estimator is a computer-based software program that calculates worldwide cost estimates for patents. It is a

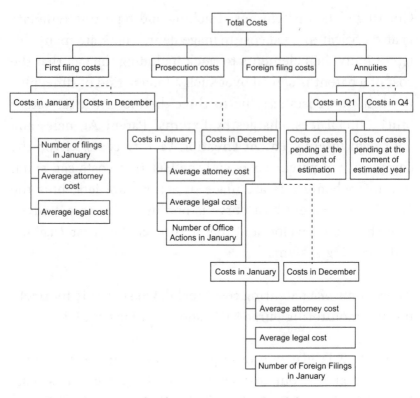

**Figure 12.2**  Example of a patenting cost breakdown structure.

straightforward tool, which utilises a regularly updated database to give you an accurate and detailed estimate of the
total cost of your patent application. The database spans the
PCT, EPO and most countries worldwide with estimates
made on the basis of the route of application, e.g., the EPO
and the countries selected. It then requires details as to the
specifics of the application, such as how many pages there
are in the application and how many pages of drawings are
included. In addition to this, several 'Yes' or 'No' questions
are asked, such as is the applicant the assignee or will there
be a late filing of assignment? The answers to these questions are combined with the information in the database

for the countries and routes selected, to form an estimate. You can then choose the format of the estimate and your options include a breakdown of the costs at each stage of filing, examination and granting of the patent, an itemised report of all the costs or in the format of a timeline.

# Hints and tips to help keep your patent costs under control

You can take some concrete steps to help better manage your patenting costs without reducing the quality of your patent or your patent portfolio:

- conduct a prior art search;
- hire a good professional patent attorney with competence in the technology area of your invention and understanding of your strategy;
- have a well developed national, regional or global filing strategy;
- trim unwanted cases;
- avoid errors and avoid being late.

Unless there is some major urgency, it makes sense that the Patent Creation Factory should carry out a prior art search. This is somewhat similar to a traditional factory inspecting components and raw material at goods-in. Although this is necessary in establishing the patentability of an invention, unnecessary costs can be avoided if such a search is performed prior to filing an application with a patent office. Should it be found that other patents or products exist that are considered too similar in nature to the invention for it to be granted patented status, you can avoid incurring the costs of the patent application procedure. For the same reason, just because a product is not on the market you should not assume that it will be considered novel or non-obvious to someone skilled in that field. Other considerations that a prior art search may address include whether the invention would be commercially successful and whether other patents would have to be 'licensed-in' in order to practice the invention.

Although it is important to keep an eye on the costs, you should not be too cost-focused when it comes to drafting the patent application. Indeed, it is well worth hiring a quality patent professional who can ensure that the application is drafted correctly and to the specific needs of the invention. This will inevitably result in a higher quality patent than if you had decided to cut corners. It is very much the case with the patent application that you get what you pay for and therefore it is essential that you allocate the necessary resources in order to protect your inventions.

If your Patent Creation Factory has in-house competence to draft a patent application you can considerably reduce the cost, but should this not be the case, it is important not to submit a poorly prepared draft patent application to an External Patent Agent or attorney. It may actually be more cost effective to allow the agent or attorney to draft the application from scratch rather than having to ask him or her to wade through a poor attempt at an application and correct every little wrong.

Choosing a good patent agent or attorney is also of significance and invariably you will need this person's help at some stage of the drafting process. Again this is not an area where you should limit your budget because it will have a negative effect on the quality of the patent application, which may increase the costs incurred at a later date. It is equally important that you provide your chosen agent or attorney with all the relevant information related to the invention. This may include descriptions and drawings prepared by the inventor, so that the application may be as detailed as possible; and remember that your failure to do this is likely to result in a reduction in quality of the granted patent and the possibility of incurring even greater costs.

Choose a patent agent or attorney with technical competence in the field of the invention, someone with whom you are comfortable working, who will find time to discuss all relevant issues and who will provide a written schedule of services. The person should also be able to give you his or her standard charges for these services, which will enable you to assess readily the costs of the services being offered before the process begins.

The cost for filing a patent application varies according to the number of countries selected and includes the fee for filing, the search fee, the translation and the costs for the arrangement of the application.

If you wish to take out protection in several countries rather than just one, inevitably the costs are going to be higher. The PCT will attempt to reduce these costs and help to postpone all expenses by 18 months, which is significantly more than that afforded by the Paris Convention. This additional time allows an essential extension, in order to assess in which countries you intend to seek protection. Subsequently, you can make a better-informed decision and potentially save the costs that could have been incurred by taking out protection in a country that you later deemed unnecessary. Although, of course, the PCT route does incur additional cost than if you were just obtaining national or regional patents, the overall gains highlighted above may make a PCT application well worth serious consideration.

One cost the PCT cannot reduce is the translation of a patent application, because this is incurred at a national level. For a PCT application to reach the regional stage before the EPO, the application must be made in English, French or German and an application in another language must be translated into one of these before it can be submitted. Prior to the award of patent status, the claims of an application must be translated into the other two languages that were not selected for the application. If the application is granted, for it to be effective in almost all of the EPC countries, the specification must be translated into the language of each country where protection is sought and this is where translation costs may start to prove expensive. The London Agreement is attempting to reduce this cost and eleven of the contracting states of the EPC have agreed to waive the above requirement so that only the claims need to be translated, rather than the full patent at the grant stage. In practice, this means that if before you had to seek protection in Sweden and Denmark, once the application was granted you would have been required to translate the entire patent into both Swedish and Danish. With the pending implementation of the London Agreement, you would now need to translate only the claims into these languages, saving the expense of employing a translator for a greater duration of time.

It is important for a business to reassess periodically whether a patent application or a granted patent should be continued with, be a candidate for trimming or be abandoned. Patent office fees are usually payable in yearly instalments, often increasing substantially towards the end of the 20 year protection period (see Table 12.1). It is therefore an unnecessary cost, should you decide that the patent is no longer considered useful, for you to continue bearing the cost of extending the life of your patent or to continue with the application. In making this decision a valuation of the usefulness of the invention is required and you may want to ask the following questions:

- Is the patent application likely to proceed to a worthwhile patent?

- Will the granted patent have direct or indirect value to your business?

- Is it possible for the patent be sold or licensed to another?

Patent annuities are the official fees that need to be paid by the patentee annually, to preserve the valid effect of the patent. Annuities must be paid to the relevant patent office on or before its expiry date, otherwise a patent right is lost, and in some countries late payment of annuity fees may cause fines to be paid in addition to the annuity fees to avoid losing your patent rights. A number of companies provide an annuity fees payment service and they can basically help you to manage the payment of annuity fees, primarily to avoid extinguishment of a patent as a result of the patentee forgetting to pay for the annuities. If you cannot identify any value with the patent, however, you perhaps need to 'trim' the case and stop paying these fees.

It may sound obvious, but avoiding errors and being on time greatly helps to keep your costs under control. A sizeable patent portfolio needs to be managed and deadlines to pay annuity payments must be met, because failure to do so may result in added expense. It is therefore important to either have some electronic reminder system in place or to hire someone to take this responsibility.

## Costs versus value

Everything has a cost and therefore you should only perform activities that create value. The key idea is that you must see patenting as an investment and not just a cost. If you have no idea of the value of your patents, there is no point investing in the activity. Why invest if there is no value?

An important aspect when considering the value of your patent portfolio is strategy. How are you planning to use patents and what is your desired outcome? These questions must be considered because value depends on need. By combining the value of your patent portfolio you can estimate how much money you have to spend on patenting, and an essential point to bear in mind is that there must be a return on investment. Therefore to judge the benefits of an investment, you must be able to define the value of it. There are two forms of value associated with a patent: direct and indirect value. The direct value of a patent covers the licensing, compensation and selling aspects whereas the indirect value can arise from competition benefit, the threat of infringement or a strategic idea. Being able to define these aspects is important because it enables you to calculate a patent's value, which in turn helps you to compile estimates.

# Summary

The management of patent costs should not be undertaken with the attitude that every cost can be reduced and indeed, adopting such an attitude will inevitably affect the quality of your patent. In certain phases it is important not to be too restrictive with your resource allocation as it is these areas that will shape the quality of your patent. Therefore, whilst it is important to be wary and not to be overly generous, being too strict will have an adverse effect. As with all things, it is about finding a balance and a carefully planned strategy will help you find this balance between costs and quality.

# 13

# Processes and tools

## Processes and tools

A process is an interrelated set of activities designed to transform inputs into outputs, which should accomplish your predefined business objectives. Processes produce an output of value to the customer, they very often span across organisational and functional boundaries and they exist whether you choose to document them or not!

> *"We should work on our process, not the outcome of the processes."* W. Edwards Deming

A process can be seen as an agreement to do certain things in a certain way and the larger your Patent Creation Factory grows and expands, the greater the need for agreements on ways of working. Processes are the memory of your factory and without them a lot of effort can be wasted by starting every procedure and process from scratch each time and possibly repeating the same mistakes. First class processes facilitate good communication between the information originator and the information receiver, because they help to set and manage expectations and the consistency of the information being given. Processes must never be allowed to become static, because they are there to serve the Patent Creation Factory and not vice versa. Ways and means to take identified improvements systematically into use should exist within your factory and well-established processes can be used as a tool to accomplish this aim. Your processes define what and how tasks are done and by whom, to ensure repeatability. They also enable you to set performance criteria and measurement, which can be utilised when identifying the source or root-cause of any problems or excessive variation.

Tool selection is best tackled once the Patent Creation Factory processes are defined; your starting point should be to define and agree the key processes and then select the tools necessary to support these processes.

Just as with a traditional factory, proper investment will enhance the factory's status as a centre of excellence for the production of patents and help achieve efficiencies within the production process. And just as a traditional factory needs various systems, tools and equipment in order to excel, the same applies to your Patent Creation Factory.

Given the costs of many of the intellectual property and patent systems and tools needed for the smooth running of your Patent Creation Factory, you need to plan these systems and tools, just as you would with any investment decision. Careful planning is the key to successful long-term investment.

Planning your systems and tools means a careful analysis of a large number of factors, such as user interface and user experience of the systems and tools, their functionality and features and their performance and reliability. You may want the ability to configure and personalise the systems and tools you choose to better suit the working environment within your Patent Creation Factory. You may also need them to interoperate with other patent specific systems and tools and with general office type systems. There is also the cost factor, both upfront and over the lifetime of the usage of the tools, plus the level of support and maintenance provided by the system and tool vendor and the quality of training and user documentation provided. The level of access control and data security may be of the utmost importance to you, or the ability to upgrade and enhance the system and tools over time and whether the system and tools are hosted in-house or externally. Last but not least, it would be advisable to research the reputation and past performance of the vendor of the systems and tools you are proposing to deploy within your Patent Creation Factory.

Planning also involves ensuring that your systems and tools support your operational model and process descriptions. Both your current processes and any future requirement needs must be taken into account in the system and tools planning, selection and deployment exercise. The systems and tools need to be flexible enough to accommodate your future requirements and must be flexible enough to support process changes and any new or varying needs of the company.

Your key external interfaces should also be analysed when planning, because certain systems and tools may help to ensure the smooth flow of information and data across these interfaces and thus foster better relations. Systems and tools that more easily facilitate the gathering and submission of ideas from the inventor community should be one of your major considerations and the reporting of key metrics to your senior management must be another. The facilitation of information flowing back and forth to External Patent Agencies is something that definitely needs to be considered when selecting systems and tools.

Some systems and tools are very general in nature and able to perform multiple functions, whereas others are very specific and focused and able to do one thing very well but nothing else. It is worthwhile giving consideration to tools that work seamlessly with others and thus avoid nonvalue 'copy and paste' type actions. Patent creation systems and tools may be purchased from a number of established vendors or developed in-house and it is worthwhile looking around and checking out the various systems and tools on offer before making any decisions. I strongly suggest that you engage the help and support of IT experts when examining, selecting and deploying patent systems and tools within your Patent Creation Factory, given the high tech nature of the systems and tools in question.

# Operational modelling/process definition work

Processes perform many useful functions within the Patent Creation Factory. They act as agreements and become part of the factory's memory, ultimately ensuring the facilitation of good communication. Processes can be an implementation tool, enabling improvements to take place and ensuring repeatability. The processes you put in place can also support a learning and developing organisation.

If your factory is organised and operating in such a manner that it has very strong functional dimensions, there is a danger that the focus will be centred on internal functions to improve their function performance and not on the overall performance of the factory. This may lead to interfaces or check points being established, based on functional borders and requiring extra hand-offs and approvals. This in turn can limit your ability to manage the whole value chain and lead to sub-optimisation of the overall factory.

A company with a strong process focus will almost certainly have to be concentrated on business targets and the customer. Your functions provide the competencies and resources that are utilised in your processes whereas your interfaces and check points are based on process borders, and you should find you have a more customer focused and responsive organisation. This should provide greater understanding and enable management of the whole value network. It enables end-to-end optimisation and facilitates the measuring of process performance.

> *"Almost all quality improvement comes via simplification of design, manufacturing ... layout, processes and procedures."* Tom Peters

There are some general principles to consider when conducting process development work. Strategy-driven process development work means creating processes that enable effective implementation of your strategy and you need to select the right organisational structures and operating models. An understanding of the output of the process is required, plus clarification of the expectations for the process performance and agreement on the rationale for conducting process development in the first place. Process development aims for compatible and optimised processes and it should enable a flexible and agile mode of operation within your Patent Creation Factory, while also improving quality. It should define quality requirements for both the output and the performance of the process, and then map those quality requirements on activity levels to related work products and ensure short feedback loops, fast responses and low corrective action costs. Continuous process development should be based on measurements and your targets should be derived from your business goals. Measures should be linked to both effectiveness and efficiency and the focus needs to be on end-to-end performance, while avoiding any sub-optimisation. Your incentives should also be linked to process metrics (see Chapter 10 for more on metrics).

Process management is one of the key issues in any organisation and you should select a skilled, clever and experienced person, who also has sociable tendencies, to help conduct this exercise and document your mode of operation and key processes. I suggest that this person must have one weakness, namely he or she must intensely dislike having to do any unnecessary work. By using this weakness the person is likely to discover the most efficient and effective way to translate the ideas flowing into your factory into good quality and valuable patents flowing out.

> *"Simplicity is the ultimate sophistication."*
> Leonardo da Vinci

Developing and implementing process improvements is not always an easy task and it is critical, before starting process definition work, that you identify all of the relevant stakeholders and ensure you get them involved in this work as early as possible. Harmonisation of the various sub-processes may take time because when you try to establish a new and different way of working, nobody is willing to change his or her own particular way of working but is usually OK for other people to change. It is also important, but sometimes difficult, to get commitment from everyone involved towards the new processes and it needs strong support from senior management within the Patent Creation Factory, and possibly even above this level, to ensure successful deployment.

# Patent systems, tools and services

In a traditional factory one needs to communicate with raw material suppliers, to understand what they have to offer and be able to manage various data flows, such as orders and payments. In a Patent Creation Factory you have to be able to have, manage and control up-to-date information on the various activities happening within the factory, such as the status of the various stages in the manufacturing process, pass rates, work-load situations, quality issues and any bottle-necks or queues. Also, you need to have, manage and control accurate information on activities being carried out by any subcontractors providing services or support to the factory. A traditional factory will have a range of systems and tools in use to help it manage all these types of issues, including tools to help monitor and improve quality, tools for budgeting and cost follow-up, and tools to help manage relationships with customers and suppliers.

Just as in a traditional factory, there are a range of tools available to help you manage the running of your Patent Creation Factory and to help the workers within your factory perform their tasks effectively and efficiently.

> *"You can't expect to meet the challenges of today with yesterday's tools and expect to be in business tomorrow."* Unknown

A simple web search will highlight the wide range of systems and tools available, and although there is a huge number of options available that can add value to your Patent Creation Factory, I suggest that great thought needs to be given to the selection of such systems and tools.

Tools that help guide the inventor through a series of steps to better describe the actual invention are very useful and some basic versions are merely templates in electronic format. There are some more advanced versions as well, which actually process the information and may even produce a printed patent application that is suitable for submission to a patent office, once it has been audited by a patent professional.

There are tools available that serve as witness for intellectual property creators. Such tools contain mechanisms that instantaneously provide digital fingerprinting, time-stamped registration of your digital files and can produce tamper-proof documentation on the integrity of your claims.

Databases are available that enable you to store all the needed information about each and every case going through your factory, from the original idea right through to granted patent and the payment of annuity fees stages, all of which are critically important to your Patent Creation Factory. Such systems help you to manage all your inventions, patent applications and granted patents, and they act as a true repository for all your records and correspondence. Databases provide you with fast access to specific data, with some of the good systems allowing you to automate parts of your internal processes. They also support your collaboration with External Patent Agencies and the various patent offices. They basically ensure that the capturing, sorting and retrieving of all your patent information is done in an efficient and cost effective manner, and when making your choice you should ensure that the system is user friendly, while providing fast access to the data you are searching for. They must allow you to extract records just as they were entered to the database and not change the history of the records, and links must be supported between different records when necessary, to provide the ability to attach or save reference material when needed.

Some systems help you manage the flow of information back and forth to the patent office. These are of particular use if you have in-house patent professionals handling your cases and they can help in avoiding errors and mistakes in the paperwork, while ensuring you do not miss any key dates in the patent application process. Search engines on the Internet are familiar to everyone browsing the Web and there are a variety of patent specific search engines available for use, some free of charge, allowing you to search through various patent databases. These can prove extremely useful, for example, when conducting prior art searches. There are also some patent search tools that are provided by national, regional and global patent offices, whereas others are commercial products on sale from specialist companies, usually with some extra 'bells and whistles' attached to give some additional value to the user. Patent search tools allow you to search through various databases looking through patent claims, the complete text from an invention disclosure, or free-form text. Patents are now considered to be one of the major sources of technological and competitive information and today's computer and Internet technologies have made it easy to access these huge information sources.

In our highly competitive business environment, patent awareness is a critical skill for business managers, engineers, researchers, inventors and consultants or anyone involved in the world of patents. Patents are an important source of technological intelligence that companies can use to gain strategic advantage and it is therefore no surprise to see better and more powerful search tools emerging. There are tools for analysing patent data and many people have begun to make increasing use of such patent information.

These tools provide analysis of the patenting activities in an industry, technology or company to ascertain or forecast the direction of technical change and to pinpoint the relative technological position of a company in a particular marketplace. Thus, the use of patent information has expanded to many different tactical and strategic business levels. Patent analysis can also have significant value for a company in understanding and predicting the development of the competitive technology landscape in its industry, and this has led to the development of powerful patent analysis tools. These tools are generally designed to help patent experts in their jobs and empower the analyst to discover previously unknown insights within patent information, which might otherwise be overlooked by just searching and viewing patent documents.

Patent mapping systems are available to allow you to truly understand the patent landscape with many of the more advanced versions allowing the patent analysis results to be displayed by visual representation, using bar graphs, polygonal line graphs, pie charts, radar charts and other charts or graphs, which are typically called 'Patent Maps'. Such visualisation is an especially effective way of representing the results of this type of patent analysis. Patent mapping is also a technique that uses patent information to create a graphical or physical representation of the relevant art pertaining to a particular technology area, which can be used to illustrate a competitor's relative patent strength. Intelligence such as this may allow you as a company to plan your research efforts strategically, evaluate the strength of your patent portfolio relative to your competitors and identify potential licensing opportunities.

A host of online tools are available that provide news and features on developments in global patent law. They provide reports on patent decisions in the courts and elsewhere, and track judgments, legislation and news within the intellectual property sector. Some are available free while others require a subscription fee.

You can also obtain patent cost estimation tools, which allow you to calculate your worldwide cost estimates for patents in advance. These can provide accurate and detailed estimates of the total costs of your patent application and there are even inventor award calculation and payment tools, although many of these tend to be company specific tools that have been created in-house.

Many more patent systems and tools are probably available as well. The growing strategic importance of intellectual property and patents means that a demand exists for better, more powerful systems and tools and for more and more applications to assist people who are directly and indirectly involved with intellectual property matters.

There may be times when search and analysis work is needed but you may not have the internal resources and expertise available in-house. Professionally made search and analysis work clearly requires good competencies and enough available resources. This is certainly the case when analysing a large amount of patents or sizeable patent portfolios, because it would be very easy to get lost in the immense amount of data available nowadays if you do not know the best methods and techniques for making searches. Well-made searches and search results are of course not the end point.

Once you have concluded your research you have to start analysing the data you have found and you may need to read through many individual patents and claims before completing the work. This complexity makes a good business case for companies to offer search and analysis services and there are indeed many such providers available to whom you can outsource this work.

# Vendor selection

One important point to remember when selecting your patent systems and tools is that processes and needs are generally unique. Therefore you should select tools based on your own particular Patent Creation Factory requirements and not just because someone else has selected and is using a particular system or tool successfully. Of course, benchmarking systems and tools against others is a very valuable exercise but please bear in mind that other companies may have totally different processes and needs and that as a result their tool selections may be totally different.

There are an increasing number of IP management system and tool providers in the marketplace, so you have a wide selection from which to choose. There are also a number of large companies involved who can offer to provide a portfolio of patent systems and tools. Many smaller companies are also involved but they are often focused on very specialist patent systems or tools that are extremely specialised and attempt to do only one task well.

It is also worth noting that changing patent creation systems, tools or tool vendors is a huge task and not something to be tackled lightly. Much time and energy must be expended in order to guarantee success.

I suggest that you need to take many of the following issues into consideration when selecting systems and tools:

- user interface design and ease of use;

- overall user experience;

- functionality;

- features;

- performance, particularly under load and stress conditions;

- architecture of the solution;

- reliability;

- ease of configuration;

- interoperability with other patent systems and tools in use within the Patent Creation Factory;

- interoperability with general office type systems and tools;

- initial costs;

- costs over time;

- support at the launch and post-launch;

- maintenance over the life-time of the tools;

- training, pre- and post-launch and by whom;

- user documentation;

- hosting, in-house or externally;

- access control;

- security such as data storage encryption, data transmission encryption, etc.;

- ability to upgrade over time and adapt to future needs;

- roadmap from the vendor showing future enhancements planned;

- manageability of the system, i.e., whether it can be administered remotely or needs local administrative support;

- interoperability with systems and tools in use across your key interfaces;

- hardware requirements;

- ease of getting good quality, useful reports out from the system or tool;

- ownership and financial status of the vendor;

- current industry reputation of the vendor;

- past performance of the vendor;

- references from other customers;

- competitive situation regarding your vendor;

- any other agreements between you and the vendor.

The scale of your Patent Creation Factory's operations will determine to some degree the importance and weight you give to each of the items in the above checklist. However, a few of the items are probably valid regardless. Many systems and tools rely upon the user interface to elevate their technical complexity to a usable product, because technology alone may not win user acceptance. The overall user experience or how the user experiences the system or tool is the key to acceptance. The user interface affects the amount of effort the user must expend in order to provide input for the system and to interpret the output of the system, and how much effort it takes to learn how to do this. The system architecture of the patent system or tool is also a key factor to consider and you need to determine the hardware, software and network capabilities. The architecture should ensure the best modularisation possible, so as to allow for easier testing, easier accommodation of new requirements at the component level and easier accommodation of new components at the system level. Protecting your information and information systems from unauthorised access, use, disclosure, disruption, modification or destruction is also a critical factor for your Patent Creation Factory. Information security is therefore one factor to consider when selecting systems and tools, encompassing the confidentiality, integrity and availability of data, regardless of the form that data may take. The costs of the systems and tools you are planning to install into your factory need to be considered, both in terms of the upfront costs as well as the costs over the expected lifetime of use.

## Summary

In response to competitive pressures and ever-changing conditions, many Patent Creation Factories are fundamentally rethinking the way they do business. It is most important to be able to link clearly your factory's production processes and organisational services to your business goals and objectives. As factories strive to keep up with ever-changing customer demands and market needs, there is a growing demand for modelling and analysis of the factories core processes, in order to capture the strategic relationships within the factory itself and with external partners and players, so as to identify areas for improvement. A process description is basically a formal representation of the structure, activities, information flow, resources, behaviours, goals, and constraints of your factory. This formal modelling of the factory should facilitate the creation of enhanced understanding of the core activities, as well as the relations that extend across the boundaries of the factory. Flow charts are easy-to-understand diagrams showing how steps in a process fit together and this makes them useful tools for communicating how processes work and clearly documenting how a particular job is done. Furthermore, the act of mapping a process out, in flow chart format, helps you clarify your understanding of the process and assists you in identifying aspects of the process that can be improved. A flow chart can therefore be used to define and analyse processes, build a step-by-step picture of the process for analysis, aid discussion and communication and identify areas for improvement (Figure 13.1).

Tool selection is best addressed once the core processes of your Patent Creation Factory are defined. Your first step should be to define and agree these key processes and then select the tools necessary to support them. Just as with a traditional factory, proper investment in systems and tools will help to ensure the Patent Creation Factory achieves the necessary

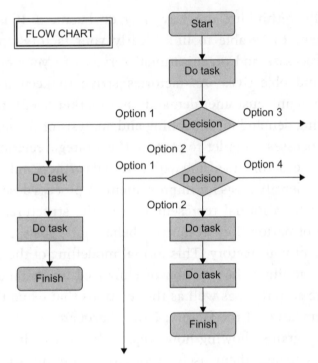

**Figure 13.1** An example of the appearance of a flowchart.

efficiencies within its production process. Given the expensive nature of many of the patent systems and tools needed for the smooth running of your Patent Creation Factory, you need to plan these systems and tools just as you would with any investment decision. Careful planning is the key to successful long-term investment.

# 14
# Benchmarking

## Introduction

Throughout this book I have written about various subjects related to the efficient and effective operation of a Patent Creation Factory, highlighting the associated issues to be considered and then discussing the options available. I have on a number of occasions indicated that there are no right or wrong options because circumstances will vary. When I wrote about organisational models, I deliberately included information on organisational change and the challenges in instigating and completing successful change projects. Benchmarking will assist you in identifying whether change is needed, what changes you should be making and when you should make these changes. Fundamentally it will provide an organisation with the courage and conviction to implement the necessary changes.

> *"Benchmarking is simply about making comparisons with other organisations and then learning the lessons that those comparisons throw up."* The European Benchmarking Code of Conduct.

Benchmarking is a process of comparing and contrasting some aspects or elements of an organisation against those of another. It is typically systematic in nature and usually reserved for critical processes, given the time and energy needed to conduct a proper and professional benchmarking exercise. The goal of any such exercise is to gain information that will help the organisation take action to improve its own performance. Benchmarking is one of the most effective means to identify improvements that can make a significant difference to your organisation, and it is certainly a useful exercise for a Patent Creation Factory to conduct and determine how well it is doing, how it compares with the industry leaders and perhaps most importantly where improvements can be made.

> *"Benchmarking is the continuous process of measuring products, services and practices against the toughest competitors or those companies recognised as industry leaders (best in class)."* The Xerox Corporation

In practice, benchmarking usually comprises comparing aspects of performance with those considered best in class, and identifying the gaps and the actions that can bring about improvements, before following through with these actions. There then needs to be a progress monitoring exercise, followed by a review of the benefits you have hopefully achieved. Benchmarking may be a one-off exercise or become a regular and repeated tool in your management toolbox. Either way it is definitely a commonly used management tool and a benchmarking culture has become embedded in successful commercial organisations as a means of seeking innovation outside the industry paradigm and as a way of keeping at the forefront of the competition.

# Benchmarking and the Patent Creation Factory

Benchmarking helps to raise awareness about the performance of your Patent Creation Factory and provides ways to identify your strengths and weaknesses, as well as any opportunities or threats. It involves learning from others, which may be somewhat of an eye-opening experience in the world of intellectual property rights (IPR), where many issues are indeed treated as confidential for very valid reasons. Benchmarking also provides encouragement in the development and application of new approaches.

Like many formal change management techniques, processes and systems, the benchmarking exercise needs to be supported by senior management to have any credibility. Depending on how the benchmarking exercise is conducted and the level of involvement of your employees in the exercise, it does allow for the greater motivation of your people. It provides a better understanding of the 'big picture' and allows your organisation to gain a broader perspective.

Benchmarking may increase collaboration and understanding between organisations. One such example is that it can increase the willingness to share solutions for common problems and build consensus about what is needed to accommodate change.

I was actively involved in a major benchmarking exercise, which definitely opened my eyes as far as the leadership and management of a Patent Creation Factory is concerned. The key learning from that exercise gave some of my colleagues and I the courage and conviction to instigate major changes in a number of areas and the motivation to see all the necessary changes right through to successful completion.

# How to conduct a benchmarking exercise

So how does one go about conducting a benchmarking exercise in the Patent Creation Factory environment and what are the first steps that need to be taken? Start by defining the scope of the exercise you wish to conduct, but be prepared for the scope and focus of the benchmarking exercise to expand or change after the initial few discussions. This certainly happened in my own benchmarking exercise experience: we initially set out to study only in-house filing, but it quickly expanded into a major organisational model and mode of operation review project, which with hindsight was the correct decision. So it is important that you and the other parties involved are given the opportunity to change the scope, or at least to tweak it.

You have to be open and willing to give out information in order to get the best back from any benchmarking exercise and in some cases you may have to accept that you will give out more than you get back. You also have to be honest and open with the information you do decide to divulge. It is therefore worthwhile to review in advance what information you are prepared to make available and to become comfortable sharing such information. This can be an uncomfortable exercise for many in the world of intellectual property, because more often than not their normal mode of behaviour is to protect information and guard it closely.

You need to decide who is going to be conducting the actual exercise. It is important you identify who is going to define the exact scope of the exercise, because it may change when other participants are approached. A number of options are available here, and the most obvious is to approach any one of the reputable consultancy firms with experience and knowledge in facilitating benchmarking exercises and getting key players to participate. There are a number of such firms who have strong IPR benchmarking expertise in terms of a good understanding of the subject matter, a strong network throughout the industry and benchmarking know-how. Other options include using companies well established in the intellectual property field with a strong network of contacts already in place, such as an intellectual property database, services and tools company. Certain patent offices may be interested in facilitating benchmarking, particularly as it may bring some benefits or lessons for them. It is also worth considering a number of the large External Patent Agencies, who may also be in a position to help. Some industry analysts may provide a solution, especially given the growing strategic importance of intangible assets. There are also a number of universities and colleges with strong skills, competencies and reputations in the area of intellectual property, who may be very interested in coordinating such an exercise. Last, but not least, you may decide to coordinate and conduct the exercise yourself by contacting other potential participants directly, although this does have some obvious drawbacks. Your decision ultimately depends on issues such as the scope of your planned benchmarking exercise, the other participants you ideally wish to see take part, your available budget and the amount of time and energy you are willing to devote to this exercise. If you do decide to get an external party to facilitate and conduct the exercise, it is important to define and agree initially who owns the benchmarking data and findings.

Who should you benchmark against? Perhaps the most obvious answer is the Patent Creation Factories in other companies. Alternatively, you may wish to benchmark against other departments in your own company such as Finance or Communications, to see how they handle the training and development of their employees or approach drafting a strategy. Benchmarking can be a relatively simple exercise if conducted internally against other company functions, but its scope will be limited, and it may not get you the answers you really need. Benchmarking against your primary competitor is a very valid comparison, but probably the most difficult to achieve as competitors are unlikely to provide a wealth of factual information allowing you to 'catch up'. In larger organisations, you may be able to benchmark against similar activities within other divisions. Ideally, you should benchmark against world-class performers: these companies are normally recognisable and will be willing to share information with a non-competitor.

Once you have made the decision to benchmark, you need to conduct some cost benefit analysis because benchmarking can be an expensive exercise, although the cost will ultimately depend on whom you choose to conduct the exercise and the scope of your benchmarking exercise. You must be willing to allocate the necessary time, energy and resources to this process in order to fully maximise what you get out of it. A limited allocation of resources will only lead to limited results. Your cost benefit analysis needs not only to gather information on the costs involved but also predict what benefits the exercise, or rather the improvement actions you take as a result of the exercise, will bring in the longer term. It is important to ensure that the cost of gathering the comparison information does not outweigh the value of the output.

# The benchmarking exercise

I recommend a five stage benchmarking process, particularly if you are involving external companies and the scope of the exercise is fairly broad:

1.  planning;

2.  forming the project team;

3.  collecting the comparison data;

4.  analysing the data for performance gaps;

5.  taking action.

The first stage in benchmarking is to plan the exercise. The objective of the planning stage is to determine what to benchmark and against whom to benchmark. This is not only to ensure that the logical deliverables of the Patent Creation Factory unit are benchmarked, but also any perceived future problem areas. You then need to select the processes to benchmark.

The second stage is to select the team members. Individuals can conduct benchmarking exercises, but in most cases these exercises are team activities, because you need to consider the workload and the knowledge requirements. A team represents the different perspectives, special skills and competences, and variety of connections that individuals can bring to the benchmarking process. The team structure will be influenced by the size and scope of the benchmarking exercise and you should ensure that the team are involved in the planning process, because the first two stages are very repetitive in nature.

The third stage involves identifying best practice companies and gathering benchmarking information about their performance and practices. Self-analysis is an essential step to effective benchmarking and one of the fundamental rules of benchmarking is to know your own processes, products and services before you attempt to understand the processes, products and services of another organisation.

> *"Benchmarking is not an exercise in imitation. It yields data, not solutions."* Jac Fitz-Enz

Once the data has been gathered, the fourth stage is identifying and analysing the gaps between best practice and your own business processes. All the collected information will then be used to identify performance gaps between benchmarking partners. When comparing the performance of companies, adjustments must be made for differences due to economies of scale, different management philosophies (e.g., outsourcing) and the operating environment between the participating companies. It may be that further discussions and study are needed with some of the other parties involved to clarify issues or to focus in on specific areas of mutual interest.

Finally, in stage five, you need to develop a strategy and action plans to close the gaps and decide what needs to be done to match best practice for any given process. You must identify tasks, responsibilities, resources and deadlines/targets for the change process and you need to prepare a budget and a cost benefit analysis, before you begin the change process. Monitor performance indicators carefully as these should highlight improved efficiencies.

People working on intellectual property matters typically love details and having a topical and authoritative benchmarking survey is a reliable way to achieve the kind of coverage that money cannot buy. When the benchmark exercise report is published, it becomes a powerful marketing tool and enables change to take place that much more easily. Overall, by circulating the findings throughout the entire Patent Creation Factory organisation, it means that everyone can continue to learn and improve, through better knowledge and understanding.

It is worth noting that often, with benchmarking exercises, the recipients of the reports are not the only beneficiaries. Benchmarking does a lot to enhance the reputation and status of the organisations that facilitate and conduct the exercise.

## My own experiences

As indicated earlier, I was actively involved in a major benchmarking exercise of our entire Patent Creation Factory, comparing and contrasting ourselves to a number of others. My colleagues and I examined our complete factory, leaving no stone unturned. My own experiences with this exercise coupled with a few other exercises of a narrower scope since then, have been generally positive and beneficial.

It is most important to establish a reason or rationale for doing a benchmarking exercise and there is usually some prompt or trigger to doing one. The usual triggers are that your organisational structure and mode of operation are not effective or efficient or there might be a major change-project taking place, forcing you to 'look in the mirror'. We spent some time at the beginning defining the scope of the exercise, as well as the looking at the reasons why we were anxious to conduct such an exercise. However, the scope changed and expanded after the initial discussions and we decided very early on in our benchmarking project that we had to employ an external company to conduct the exercise.

One important step we took was to inform all our employees about the benchmarking exercise prior to it starting so that everything was out in the open; we also gave our people an opportunity to participate actively in the project. This is a critical issue in my opinion because otherwise even good intentions are not construed as such, particularly if kept secret or hidden away. Openness and honesty will pay dividends in the long run.

We identified the information we were prepared to make available to the company coordinating and conducting the actual exercise, as well as to the other companies participating. We opened up our entire organisation to the external company conducting the benchmarking exercise, inviting them to interview anyone within the company as well as providing them access to detailed internal reports and data so as to gain a true picture of our current state. This issue about openness and honesty needs to be discussed very early on in the project to ensure that everyone is aware of what is involved and is generally comfortable with this approach.

We needed to determine who else we wanted to be involved in the exercise and there were decisions to be made about with whom we wanted to be compared and contrasted. We discussed such options as getting the top 10 companies in the world involved, having a mixture of large established companies and small start up companies involved, selecting companies from different countries and regions and having companies from very diverse industries involved.

Simply discovering the identities of the other companies who agreed to be involved in the benchmarking exercise, and how they had reacted to the initial approach to participate, provided some very interesting insights. Had they been quick to climb on board and were they enthusiastic? Were they contributing ideas as to what could be included into the exercise and did they try to widen or narrow the scope of the exercise?

Ask yourself what the participating companies are hoping to achieve from the exercise and what they are actually going to get out of the exercise. They may wish to get a summary of the findings and/or a copy of the complete final report containing data and analysis. On the other hand, they may be expecting payment for agreeing to participate. This issue needs to be discussed and resolved at a very early stage in the project to ensure that at the end of the exercise there are no disagreements about specific deliverables between the bench-marked companies.

Great care had to be taken with the wording and terminology being used as it does differ from company to company, and we had to be prepared to explain our terminology in simple terms throughout the project. There may also be wide differences between the key technologies of the benchmarked companies and they may use different classification systems to identify technology areas.

In our benchmarking exercise a project steering group was established, which met regularly throughout the project to review progress and to address any open issues in a timely manner. This was also important because we had to ensure that there were adequate resources (people, time, funding) for the benchmarking team to achieve its goal. Just as with any project team you need to give consideration to the team structure and dynamics and the personalities involved, as well as the skills and competencies, knowledge and experience that each member brings to the steering group. This will help you with guiding and directing the overall project.

We spent a lot of time reviewing the final data and the key lessons, so as to determine the correct improvement actions needed. Your benchmarking exercise will fail if you do not take on board the key lessons learnt and then take some concrete actions to implement the recommended changes. We followed up on a one-to-one basis with a few of the other companies participating in the formal benchmarking exercise, prompted by some of the comparison data. We also maintained a good relationship with the company who conducted the benchmarking exercise and we have used this as an opportunity to discuss with them the positive changes we made and the benefits these brought.

# Benchmarking a Patent Creation Factory

So what can you benchmark when it comes to the world of Patent Creation Factories? Basically it is possible to compare and contrast any and all aspects of your company that are of value and interest. This may include such issues as organisational models and modes of operation, the patenting processes from idea through to granted patent or the effectiveness and efficiency of the factory and your intellectual property systems, plus the tools that you use in the factory. You may decide to target cost management practices, patent quality and filing strategies or the skills and competencies of your people. Or you may wish to look at work allocation, in-house versus External Patent Agencies, and the External Patent Agency management practices. Maybe you want to compare and contrast the relationships with your inventor community and the processes you use for PULLING ideas from outside your company, or your intellectual property relationships with universities, suppliers, partners and customers.

## Summary

This chapter has introduced the important subject of benchmarking as far as a Patent Creation Factory is concerned. In simple terms, it is an exercise to compare yourself with others in order to make improvements and if it is a successful exercise it should, ideally, lead to improvements in your patenting cost, your patent quality and the effectiveness and efficiency of your Patent Creation Factory processes.

I have provided examples of how to benchmark and how to deploy your key findings. The central point to this chapter is that it aims to advise the reader that once the Patent Creation Factory is established, benchmarking should be considered as an effective way to test and measure its success, because it enables a comparison to be made with competing companies or other organisations.

Benchmarking is definitely one of the most commonly used management tools. A benchmarking culture has become embedded in successful commercial organisations as a means

of seeking innovation outside of the industry paradigm and is
a way of keeping at the forefront of the competition.

> *"You know you need to benchmark, but you are just too busy. Well if you don't benchmark and then implement improvements based on it, you will find yourself out of business. Then you'll have plenty of time to benchmark, but it won't matter."* John Reh

# 15

# Changes

## Introduction

As this is the penultimate chapter, I feel it is the best place to bring to your attention some of the changes happening in the patenting world. Inevitably, there are an abundance of initiatives taking place worldwide and to mention them all would be impossible and frankly, unnecessary. Instead, I have opted to hand pick a variety of examples, some of which will undoubtedly have a greater effect than others, just to give you an idea on how the patenting world is evolving. Some of the changes described below are actually happening whereas others are still at the discussion and debate stage.

> *"The dogmas of the quiet past are inadequate to the stormy present. The occasion is piled high with difficulty and we must rise with the occasion. As our case is new, so we must think anew and act anew."* Abraham Lincoln

The chapter looks first of all at the concept of a European Community Patent – an initiative that aims to improve the current European patent system – and examines the reasons behind the need for an alternative system, following its development in trying to become more than an idea. The chapter then considers the growth of the North East Asian countries and how their development is signalling a significant shift in the distribution of dominance within the patent world. It identifies the challenges that patent offices now face in the light of increased applications, leading us nicely into the Patent Prosecution Highway pilot scheme, one solution (currently being trialled) to the issue of an increased workload. I then consider changes in the US patent system, citing the case of *KSR vs Teleflex* as an example of how the US system is undergoing change, and this is followed with an insight into innovation developments in the business community, drawing your attention to one particular IBM-led initiative. The chapter then explores an initiative led by the World Business Council for Sustainable Development (WBCSD) related to environmental patents. Finally, I explore the report on Future Scenarios, a European Patent Office (EPO) project that attempts to provide several scenarios of what the patent world may look like in 20 years time, a fitting end to our chapter.

# European regional initiatives

For many years now there have been proposals regarding a European Community patent, however nothing has yet materialised. The European Commission recently set out its thoughts on the future of the European Patent System, its desire to make the idea of a Community patent a reality and to improve the existing patent litigation system by making it cheaper and more accessible.

> *"Europe's patent system is considerably more expensive than the US and Japanese Systems. A European patent designating thirteen countries is eleven times more expensive than a US patent and thirteen times more than a Japanese patent."* Charlie McCreevy, European Union Internal Market and Services Commissioner

The clear reason for such a difference in cost between a European patent as against a Japanese or US patent is that the US and Japan are sovereign countries and as such their systems are nationalised. A patent, when granted, extends to the boundaries of their country and is enforced by their state judiciary. Europe, on the other hand, is not a single country, it is a collection of countries and therefore has to confront issues concerning linguistic differences and the sovereignty of individual states. The latter is particularly important. States are sovereign powers of their own borders and they require their domestic laws to be met and enforcement to take place within their domestic judicial system. For the costs to be reduced comparatively to that of Japan and the US, Europe must find a way to remove these obstacles and act in a state of unity.

The concept of a Community patent is one that tries to overcome these hurdles, namely the idea of one single patent to cover the whole European Community rather than a collection of nationalised patents. However, there are problems to overcome with issues related to translation and enforcement. The Commission has tried to address these problems, first, through the London Agreement, which essentially provides that an application need be in only one of the official languages of the Community (English, German or French), and second, through the European Patent Litigation Agreement (EPLA), which attempts to commit all member states of the European Community to a single integrated judicial system that would include uniform rules of procedure and a common appeal court. However, the London Agreement still requires ratification and the concept of a single judicial body has encountered problems whereby its competence has been called into question. It seemed that the concept of a Community patent was dead and buried, but persistence from the Community institutions to push it through have led to hopes that it will be a reality one day.

## Developments in the Far East

The 2007 edition of the Patent Report of the World Intellectual Property Office (WIPO) shows that on a worldwide scale, filings of patent applications are increasing at an average rate of nearly 5 % per year. Perhaps unsurprisingly, but nevertheless significantly, the highest growth rates have been recorded by the North East Asian countries, in particular the Republic of Korea and China.

The patent offices with the most patents filed are Japan, the US, China, Korea and the European Patent Office and these, added together, account for over three-quarters of all patents filed. The Patent Office in China saw a remarkable increase of almost a third more applications than the previous year, making it the third biggest recipient of patent filings. However, it still has a long way to go to break into the top two where the US and Japan account for almost half of all patents granted. Moreover, the figures show promisingly that many newly industrialised countries are beginning to embrace the patent system.

> *"We have witnessed a significant increase in the use of the patent system internationally in recent years . . . while the use of the system remains highly concentrated, we are seeing a historic evolution in the geography of the innovation. With increased patenting activity in newly industrialising and emerging countries, we expect the pattern of ownership of patent rights worldwide will become more diversified over the coming years."*
> Dr Kamil Idris, WIPO Director General

The report affirms the growth of the North East Asian countries, widely expected by many because the region has significantly increased its share of worldwide patenting, both as a source of patent applications and as a target of non-resident patent applications from outside the region. In the 10 year period between 1995 and 2005, resident patent filing doubled in Korea and increased more than eight fold in China. The Patent Office in China boasts the highest growth rate for resident filings (an improvement of over 40 %) as well as non-resident filings (almost 25 %).

> *"Countries in North East Asia will most likely continue to challenge their counterparts elsewhere. A few years ago they took the patent world by surprise, but it is now very much the expectation that countries like China and the Republic of Korea will continue their rapid development in innovation, one indicator of which is the number of patent applications filed."*
> Mr Francis Gurry, WIPO Deputy Director General

However, the increased number of applications has raised questions as to whether the patent offices can deal with this influx of demand. Both the US and Japan each had almost one million applications pending in 2006, although in the case of the latter this can be attributed to changes in the time limit for request for examination, which has temporarily increased the workload of the examination.

## Cooperation between patent offices

The Patent Prosecution Highway (PPH) scheme is a pilot programme that has been adopted by the US, Japanese and UK patent offices. Its purpose is to provide applicants with a method to fast-track their application, by recognising the results of the examination that has already been conducted by another intellectual property office. Originally trialled by the US and Japanese in the summer of 2006, its success has led to the UK conducting similar agreements with both states the following year.

> *"Patent users worldwide want offices to cooper-*
> *ate more effectively. Our collective goal is to reduce*
> *duplication of work, speed up processing and improve*
> *quality... this pilot project with the UK builds on*
> *work with the Japanese Patent Office and contri-*
> *butes to a more rational international patent system."*
> Jon Dudas, US under Secretary of Commerce for Intellectual Property
> and Director of the United States Patent and Trademark Office

The initiative was born as a result of a need to speed up the examination procedure and reduce the overall workload of many patent offices, due to the increased numbers of applications. Research showed that much of this workload could be reduced with the introduction of an initiative reducing the cross-national duplication of effort. At the same time concerns were voiced that any proposal should not come at the expense of the quality of the patents granted, although the overwhelming response was that by reducing the workload on the patent offices, quality could actually improve.

> *"The pilot project represents an important first step*
> *towards our goal of reducing duplication of search-*
> *ing through work sharing... as patent offices through-*
> *out the world deal with an ever increasing workload,*
> *we must find ways to streamline processing and avoid*
> *redundancy through cooperative efforts such as the*
> *Patent Prosecution Highway."*   Jon Dudas, US under
> Secretary of Commerce for Intellectual Property and Director of
> the United States Patent and Trademark Office

The basic concept is that where an applicant has already received an examination report in Japan, the US or the UK, indicating that at least one of his or her claims is patentable, the applicant may request an accelerated examination of the application in the other two offices. Subsequently, the intellectual property office of each state benefits from the work already performed by its counterpart. The pilot scheme aims to measure the demand from applicants for this option of hastening the examination of their patent application, while quantifying the relative gains in quality and efficiency that are expected. Although the PPH is still no more than a pilot scheme, it is indeed showing promising signs.

> *"The Patent Prosecution Highway helps both offices in their goal of stimulating and rewarding invention and innovation and is a further step towards a global patent prosecution network."* Lord Triesman, Parliamentary under Secretary of State for Intellectual Property & Quality

## Changes in US patent law

The US case of *KSR vs Teleflex* has had a significant impact on the patentability of inventions in the US. Essentially, Teleflex argued that KSR's products infringed one of its patents, while KSR countered that the patent should not have been granted in the first place, because it failed to satisfy the obviousness test. The relevant legislation provided that an invention could not be patented if a 'person having ordinary skill in the art' would consider it obvious.

The Supreme Court of the US found that the Federal Circuit had failed to adequately apply this provision as their conception of obviousness was too narrow when they required a challenging party to prove there was a 'teaching, suggestion or motivation' linking it to the prior art. Subsequently, a sufficiently stringent standard had not been applied.

> *"The results of ordinary innovation are not the subject of exclusive rights under the patent laws. Were it otherwise, patents might stifle rather than promote the progress of useful arts."* Justice Anthony Kennedy

The immediate effect of this ruling was that the Teleflex patent was invalidated; its secondary effect, however, has proved much more significant, in that it acted as a signal that the Federal Circuit, going forward, will have to take a stricter stance when determining a patent's obviousness. However, these issues are still being debated within the US Court system, and so at this moment it is unclear exactly what the future may hold in this area.

# Patent initiatives by individual companies

Inspired by a two-month, online forum involving dozens of experts, in September 2006 IBM formalised a new corporate policy governing the creation and management of patents. The policy is designed to foster integrity, a healthier environment for innovation and a mutual respect for intellectual property rights (IPR). IBM has encouraged others in the patent community to adopt similar policies and practices more stringently than currently required by law. The key elements of the new policy, which applies everywhere that IBM does business, are as follows:

- Patent applicants are responsible for the quality and clarity of their patent applications.

- Patent applications should be available for public examination.

- Patent ownership should be transparent and easily discernible.

- Pure business methods without technical merit should not be patentable.

*"The centrepiece of this policy and our actions to support it, is based on the principles that patent quality is a responsibility of the applicant. These principles are as relevant in emerging regions of the world as they are in more mature economies. IBM is holding itself to a higher standard that any law requires because it's urgent that patent quality is improved, to both stimulate innovation and provide greater clarity for the protection and enforcement of intellectual property rights."* Dr John E. Kelly III, IBM Senior Vice President for Technology and Intellectual Property

# WBCSD initiative with environmental patents

The World Business Council for Sustainable Development (WBCSD) and IBM, in partnership with Nokia, Pitney Bowes and Sony, launched, in early 2008, the Eco Patent Commons Initiative, a collection of patents pledged by member companies for the free use of anyone to make it easier and faster to innovate, collaborate and implement industrial processes that improve and protect the environment. The patents will be housed on a dedicated, public web site hosted by the WBCSD.

Patents pledged to the Eco Patent Commons may include innovations specifically focused on environmental solutions, such as new technology for solar panels or new methods for groundwater remediation. Patents may also include innovations in manufacturing or business processes where the solution also provides an environmental benefit. For example, a company may pledge a patent for a manufacturing process that also reduces hazardous waste generation or energy or water consumption, or a procurement or logistics solution may reduce fuel consumption.

Examples of the environmental benefits that pledged patents may provide include energy conservation or improved energy or fuel efficiency, pollution prevention (source reduction, waste reduction), use of environmentally preferable materials or substances, reduced use of water or materials, and increased recycling ability.

Companies utilising the Eco Patent Commons will receive free access to intellectual assets they can leverage to improve the environmental aspects of their operations, helping them become efficient and operate in a more environmentally sustainable manner. The Commons also provides a way for companies facing a challenge that may have environmental impact, to connect and collaborate with companies that have had success in meeting similar challenges in a way that is protective of the environment.

For member companies sharing patents, the Eco Patent Commons provides a catalyst for further innovation and can facilitate potential new opportunities for collaboration between the patent user and the company pledging the patent. It is also an efficient channel by which companies can share their innovative solutions.

> *"The Eco Patent Commons provides a unique and significant leadership opportunity for business to make a difference – sharing their innovations and solutions in support of sustainable development."*  Bjorn Stigson, President of the WBCSD

Membership in the Eco Patent Commons is open to all companies pledging one or more patents. The founding companies and the WBCSD are inviting other interested companies to become members and participate in this initiative promoting innovation and collaboration to improve and protect the planet.

# The WIPO WorldWide Academy

In March 1998, the Director General of the World Intellectual Property Organization (WIPO), Dr. Kamil Idris, founded the WIPO WorldWide Academy in response to a demand for knowledge and skills in intellectual property (IP). It serves as a centre of excellence in teaching, training and research in IP. Its programmes are designed to cater to different target audiences: inventors and creators; business managers and IP professionals; policy makers and government officials of IP institutions; diplomats and representatives; and students and teachers of IP and the civil society.

Its objectives are achieved through five core programmes: professional training, distance learning, policy development, teaching and research. The tailor-made programmes, including its distance learning with more than 40000 participants since its inception in 1999, benefit large numbers of people from all walks of life.

The Academy seeks to stay continuously innovative by offering new programmes to keep up with the ever-changing IP landscape. It also aims to promote international cooperation for enhancing IP human capital, through global networking with stakeholders and partners.

The WIPO WorldWide Academy has a number of programmes in place. Distance learning is an alternative and a complement to traditional training methods, in order to make course materials accessible to large audiences worldwide. The Policy Development Program offers courses, which form part of the

WIPO Training Program and additionally offers a variety of other new and innovative courses. The WIPO Training Program seeks to provide general and specialised training for senior officials in the field of IP. The Policy Development Program more particularly focuses on IP information sharing; orientation and training for decision-makers, policy-advisers and other senior officials involved in the protection, administration and enforcement of IPR.

The Professional Training Program offers courses that are part of the WIPO Training Program, and seeks to provide general and specialised training for professionals in the field of IP. The programme is carried out at WIPO Headquarters and in partnership with governments and specialised institutions, such as national and regional IP offices, where participants receive practical training. The various courses offered by the Professional Training Program provide basic or specialised training on the law, administration and enforcement of IPR and the use and dissemination of industrial property documentation and information. The courses cover all fields of IP: industrial property, copyright and related rights.

The WIPO WorldWide Academy also offers a range of Executive Programs and these are geared towards developing IP skills and competencies in business organisations. Drawing on WIPO's vast expertise and resources, and a carefully selected group of eminent academics and experts from renowned business schools, major global corporations, professional bodies and business consultants, the WIPO WorldWide Academy offers a unique interdisciplinary learning experience in the theory and practice of international IP management.

WIPO has established formal partnerships with a number of universities and IP teaching and education is now a common goal for many universities, which share similar problems. Cooperation among those universities is necessary. During the past few years, several universities have established strategic alliances (not only in the same country but also cross-border partnerships) leading to the exchange of lecturers and students and the sharing of useful information. Some universities have agreed on the mutual recognition of degrees.

Last, but not least, the WIPO WorldWide Academy offers a summer school on IP matters. The objective of the Summer School is to provide an opportunity for senior students and young professionals to acquire a deeper knowledge of IP and to gain an appreciation of IP as a tool for economic, social, cultural and technological development and the role WIPO plays in the global administration of IP.

# European Patent Office project looking at future scenarios

The European Patent Office (EPO) commissioned a two-year project (known as 'Scenarios for the Future') to interview the key players from the scientific, economic, political and legal domains to gain a consensus as to how the IP world may look in 20 years time. Four scenarios were developed from their answers, which they called:

- Market rules

- Whose game?

- Trees of knowledge

- Blue skies

The first scenario ('Market rules') is one where business becomes the main motive behind patent protection and as companies increase their investment in patent protection, to increase their market share, they will subsequently increase their share value. Because multinational corporations play a dominant role as a result of their huge patent portfolios, they will also play an influential role in driving the patent agenda so that issues such as patent trolling and anti-competitive behaviour become top of the agenda. However, the increasing scope of subject matter increases the number of patents being granted and the abundance of new players makes it harder to enforce rights as a backlog of claims pile up. The system gets crushed under the weight of litigation, highlighting the need for new forms of IP protection and new mechanisms to deal with such a high volume of claims.

The second scenario ('Whose game?') is one where the developed world, which has failed to use its IP to maintain its technological superiority, has to embrace new entrants into the system. China and India in particular became more powerful and began to shape the system to meet their own needs and in the process they were able to establish an economic advantage. However, the two respective systems progress at different speeds with the Chinese adopting the Western model of immediate high standards while India, concerned about potential negative economic and social effects, adopts a much slower progression. Furthermore, the two economies have different natures with the patent system fitting more naturally to China's manufacturing economy rather than India's services industry. This has resulted in India pursuing new forms of IP protection that ultimately represent its interests better. This kind of fragmentation in the IP world makes enforcement more difficult, and meanwhile much of the developing world becomes further excluded from the system resulting in them working within a 'communal knowledge' paradigm.

Another possible scenario ('Trees of knowledge') is one where society is considered to be the main driver and this can occur in a social context where trust of the intellectual system is low and, consequently, criticism is high. Protection is seen as an anti-competitive means to benefit bigger companies while hindering the progression of smaller companies. Protection of pharmaceutical goods comes under the spotlight, because patent protection is deemed as making them more expensive and limiting their provision. Furthermore, the open source movement, which has become significantly more popular, holds the belief that patents block the use of technology and are subsequently demanding the freedom to access entertainment and knowledge with greater ease. There is active debate as to the interest of the people versus the interest of businesses, particularly in how to ensure that knowledge remains a common good while still acknowledging the legitimacy of rewarding innovation: the outcome of this will ultimately come down to the strength of the open source movement.

The final scenario ('Blue skies') sees technology as the main driver. Complex technologies are seen as the key to solving problems such as climate change and the IP needs of these technologies will conflict with their older counterparts, requiring the patent system to respond by abandoning the one-size-fits-all system and creating new IPR for the new technologies.

What is clear is that no matter which scenario turns out to become practice, new forms of IP and new mechanisms will be required to deal with more advanced technologies, changing the global markets and their subsequent needs to deal with increased numbers of patents. Although no one can predict with 100 % certainty what the future entails, these scenarios provide key illustrations as to what we can expect based on current trends and conceptions.

## Summary

It is clear that the patent world is evolving at quite a speed and I have tried to highlight relatively recent developments so that when published, these examples will not be too outdated. Inevitably though, newer developments will head the agenda and potentially change the entire nature of the patent world.

You can keep up to date with the changes occurring in the world of patents thanks to a number of reliable avenues. Intellectual property newsletters, often containing information and analysis on changes, are available from many established patent agencies and IP organisations. Global, Regional and National Patent Offices maintain well-designed, informative web sites, which again contain information on changes taking place or under discussion. The mainstream media are beginning to take IP and patent issues much more seriously in recent times and it is not uncommon for coverage to be given to many of the issues discussed in this chapter, as well as many other similar types of patent related developments. A host of seminars and workshops are held around the globe on IP and patent related topics, often with presenters and lecturers drawn from leading companies and organisations in this field. The Internet is another very useful source of information on such matters, although some care needs to be taken to ensure that the information you obtain is based on well-researched and informed opinion.

Several important issues have been raised in this chapter. Firstly the patenting world is experiencing greater numbers of applications every year and this is threatening the current worldwide patent systems that are in place, because they were not necessarily built to deal with such demand. The two solutions to this problem are either to apply the patentability requirements more stringently or to adapt the patent offices to deal with the influx of applications more efficiently. Initiatives such as the Patent Protection Highway are being trialled as a means to help reduce the duplication of examinations between countries. Second, the reduction of costs will always be at the forefront of motives for both innovation and change and this can be seen in the European Community Patent initiative, which attempts to reduce the cost of filing a European application to a charge more similar to that of the US and Japanese Patent Offices. IP initiatives by individual companies or industry organisations are also worth monitoring, given the part they play.

The future scenarios predicted by those interviewed in the EPO project paint a picture of how the patenting world may look in the years to come. Although the report proves interesting reading, the speed and unpredictability with which the field of patents is evolving makes it highly unlikely that anyone will be able to predict with 100 % precision what the future holds in store. What is clear is that with greater numbers of applications and patents being granted, the patent world is becoming increasingly important.

*"In times of change, learners inherit the Earth, while the learned find themselves beautifully equipped to deal with a world that no longer exist."* Eric Hoffer

# 16

# Conclusion

## Conclusion

Starting this book was relatively easy, but finishing it has been an interesting challenge. Each time I spoke to someone during the research the ending changed a little, until it was completely different from what I had expected, but far, far better.

> *"We will be judged by what we finish, not by what we start."* Anonymous

I was most fortunate when writing this book to be working in a very innovative and creative environment, surrounded by many inventive people. There was an atmosphere within the company that permitted people to have the necessary freedom to stray from what might be normal or ordinary everyday work.

This project did not start with the objective of writing a book but rather it started as an exercise to tidy up my own notes. I have been very fortunate to have been involved in a number of interesting and challenging patent projects over a number of years and I wanted to gather my notes together in a proper and professional manner. These notes covered such projects as a major benchmarking exercise, a fundamental organisational change project and the deployment of new patent systems and tools across the entire factory. There were also projects involving critical changes to the interface with our inventor community and dramatic changes to the management of our relationships with our External Patent Agencies, plus many more.

> *"The power of the word is real whether or not you are conscious of it. Your own words are the bricks and mortar of the dreams you want to realize. Behind every word flows energy."* Sonia Choquette

## Patents are of importance

The importance of patents is growing, often equalling or surpassing the value of physical assets for a company. The state of the intellectual property (IP) of a company will help to determine its share and corresponding influence on the market. The size and quality of your portfolio will have a direct impact on several factors, such as the reputation of your company, the level of returns on investments and your access to the market, among others.

The volume of patent applications and granted patents has been increasing in recent years. As companies have now begun to realise just how important patent rights are in the modern business environment, it is unsurprising that this pattern has emerged.

However, there is a complexity associated with the patenting process. The process is by no means simple and there are various steps or stages in the process. The patenting language and terminology is often not easily understood and it can also be a relatively expensive exercise. The reason for such complexity, in particular in the application and granting stages, is to ensure that the patents that do get through are of the utmost quality and provide protection only to the extent necessary.

Good management and leadership is a requirement, in order to have a successful Patent Creation Factory and you will need to focus on the organisational structure and mode of operation for your factory to be successful. This requires clear management and leadership, such as conveying clear direction and meaningful vision in all parts of the factory, followed by deploying and controlling your resources, whether they are your people and money, or your physical and intangible assets.

> *"The major challenge for leaders in the twenty-first century will be how to release the brain power of their organisations."* Warren Bennis

# The factory analogy

The factory analogy used throughout the book stems from the notion that patent creation should not be seen as some simple legal process but rather as a core activity of 'creating' patents, just like a factory creating products.

The basic idea is that if you wish to create patents as effectively as possible, you should then see the process as similar to that of a factory production line, in which the end result is the granted patent. Patent creation should be treated in much the same way as you would handle product development and granted patents should be treated in the same way as you would handle a finished product.

Patent creation is an activity that involves interfacing to the inventor community, gathering inventions, analysing them, making decisions and then filing and prosecuting cases. It can be seen as a virtual factory, producing quality patents at the end of the production line for others to then utilise.

However, it is not an isolated factory disconnected from the company or the business environment, it is a factory well connected to those developing strategies. Actively linked to the inventor community, it should take pride in raising awareness of IP and patents throughout the company and it should continuously grow and develop its people, processes and tools. Furthermore, it will do the basics well, such as harvesting inventions, reviewing those inventions and filing and prosecuting those considered of value, ultimately to obtain good quality granted patents.

As leader and manager of this Patent Creation Factory, you will need to formulate a long-term strategy for the factory, on the basis of the overall IP strategy and the overall company strategy. You will then have to identify the competencies needed to achieve the strategic objectives and targets and ensure team and individual targets are in line with the strategic objectives of the factory. You will be required to monitor actively the source, volume and quality of the raw material (inventions) coming into the factory and to participate in factory process and tool development, while managing the budget in a professional business manner. All these factors will ultimately ensure the quality of the patents produced within your factory. Patent creation clearly involves an array of activities of which you need to be aware, with the overall objective and ultimate goal being to create good quality patents.

The importance of patenting an invention is clear to see and failing to do so may prove catastrophic to a business. Patenting an invention is a decision involving the consideration of many factors, such as the cost and relative gains. Therefore, one should not patent every invention: not only would this be a costly mistake but it would also reduce the effectiveness of the patent system. Indeed, the requirements of novelty, inventive step and industrial applicability act as a mechanism to preserve the quality of patents.

In a factory, you begin with the raw materials needed to make the final product. Should the product be made with one of its components missing, the final product will not be the same as the others. It will be of a lower quality, it may not do what it was designed to do and as a consequence it may result in customer dissatisfaction. All these factors apply to patent creation.

Many benefits arise from patenting an invention and companies see high future value in patents and continue to invest in them. Today, it is more than just a few patent owners protecting inventions; the IP and patent landscape is rapidly changing. Patents are big business and IP and patent strategy is becoming central for business strategy and one of the determining factors for the success of a company.

# Steps to success

Step one is the creation of a strategic plan. You may think that strategy is something theoretical or impractical, but in general this is not the case and also not the case with IP and patents. Just like in a factory, there needs to be a plan that is followed when deciding what to produce and when. It is best if the strategy you create is relatively clear and straightforward because this increases the chance of successful implementation and the best strategies are usually those that deal only with the most important issues. The strategy and top level action plan will need to cascade down to individual level, so that everyone knows what he or she is doing, and always have some degree of flexibility built into your strategy. The strategy for your Patent Creation Factory needs to be in alignment with the overall IP strategy and the overall company strategy. Once developed, the strategy needs to be communicated to the factory and beyond.

In order to embark upon the journey of patent creation you must appreciate patents and how they work. You must also understand the rights and obligations that accompany them otherwise you have no foundation upon which to build your Patent Creation Factory. A patent is an exclusive right granted for an invention. Patents are generally intended to cover products or processes that contain new functional or technical aspects. They are therefore concerned with how things work, what they do, how they do it, what they are made of or how they are made. Patent protection means that the invention cannot be commercially made, used, distributed or sold without the patent owner's consent and this protection is granted for a limited period, generally 20 years from filing. A patent owner has the right to decide who may, or may not, use the patented invention. The patent owner may give permission to use the invention or license other parties to use the invention on mutually agreed terms. The owner may also sell the right to the invention to someone else, who then becomes the new owner of the patent.

Ideas, ideas and more ideas!!! Innovation acts as the raw material of your patent factory. The quality of your ideas will therefore have the most direct outcome on the success of what you have set out to achieve. It is therefore important, if you wish to create a patent portfolio, that you ensure not only that your ideas are of the highest quality, but also that you have a steady supply of them. Creativity and innovation are key elements to survival and profitability in any business environment and markets are constantly demanding new products, with better designs and more features at a lower price. Consequently, the effective management of innovation is a vital component of any successful business. Innovation starts with thinking differently. It is a process of questioning, experimenting, learning and adapting and it requires an appetite for risk, a willingness to question, an open mind to look at data without a predetermined conception and perhaps most importantly, patience.

The fundamental core steps in the patenting process need to be fully understood. By breaking down the process into the simple stages of application, filing, preliminary examination and search, publication, substantial examination and search, grant and maintenance, you should now have a better idea of the requirements and stages of the patenting process that collectively may have otherwise seemed a daunting task. Indeed, you will realise by now that the process is long, costly and sometimes frustrating. However, you should have taken this into account as part of your initial strategy, and by deciding to patent you have obviously decided that the process is worthwhile. Having decided to patent your invention, this is the part of the process where you can watch the patent coming together. In our factory, it is the equivalent of starting out with the raw materials and step-by-step, observing a different part of your product being assembled. At the end of this process you will have your fully assembled goods and you will have your patent!

There are a number of critical interfaces and relationships to develop and maintain, in order to ensure that a patent factory is successful in creating the highest quality patents. The Patent Creation Factory cannot exist in isolation. You therefore need to look outside the factory walls at these critical groups and identify ways and means to ensure all groups work together towards a common goal. Now, depending upon the scale of your particular patent factory, the organisational model you adopt, the processes you put in place, the nature of your business plus probably a number of other factors, your Patent Creation Factory's external interfaces may be slightly different from what is described here. Regardless, you will have a number of critical external interfaces and relationships to manage and develop, in order to ensure that your patent factory is successful in creating good quality and valuable patents. You will need to identify the external interfaces that exist in your particular scenario, gain insight and understanding of each of these interfaces and determine what is needed to make all these interfaces work well. It is also worth noting that your external interfaces are very likely to change over time, thanks perhaps to company level or IP level organisational changes, changes to your Patent Creation Factory strategy and top-level action plans, or influences and changes in the external world.

How are you going to organise and structure your internal Patent Creation Factory so that you do so in an effective and efficient manner? The book has outlined the factors that you need to consider when deciding how to organise, structure and operate your factory. It has also provided you with examples of organisation models, including diagrams, which outline possible ways to organise, plus advice on how to overcome the issues and problems that may arise. You can select from a variety of organisational models and there are pros and cons associated with each model. The models are not by any means mutually exclusive and it may well be that the organisation model you select consists of elements of more than one of the models illustrated. The organisational structure that best suits your circumstances today may not be the best option for you in the future, as your Patent Creation Factory develops and matures, so it is most likely that your organisational structure will change over time.

Many of the organisational models involve doing some of the work outside the walls of your factory, and in fact a few of the models suggest outsourcing all or almost all the activities of your Patent Creation Factory. There are IP and patent specific companies capable of handling parts of or all the tasks of a Patent Creation Factory on your behalf. Their capabilities range from analysis of the novelty and patentability of an idea, through to the actual drafting of cases, filing the appropriate paperwork with the patent offices, prosecution of cases, including handling office actions and doing translation work. They will also undertake filing of foreign cases with the appropriate patent offices, conduct detailed searches and examinations and all tasks right up until the grant stage. There are also external companies who will manage the payment of annuity fees on your behalf. Involvement of External Patent Agencies in the operation of your Patent Creation Factory is basically just a means of buying certain work results from third parties. Your long-term goal should be to have an optimised number of carefully selected External Patent Agencies that are managed in a unified way and with whom your relationship is constantly under development. To ensure that you are managing and developing these relationships, it is worthwhile putting some fundamental elements in place. Professional frame agreements should be in place between you and your External Patent Agencies and instructions issued to clarify how work tasks are to be ordered. The workflow between you and the External Patent Agencies also needs management and cost and quality controls are of paramount importance. However, having frame agreements and pricing models in place is really only setting the foundations. Much more is needed to truly manage your External Patent Agencies and to establish a long term, mutually beneficial and professional working relationship.

A number of essential metrics must be considered and assessed in order to monitor and measure the performance of your Patent Creation Factory. Such metrics enable calculations and comparisons to be made of the factory, in order to establish whether the factory is running effectively and efficiently and in line with targets. It is essential to decide upon the correct measures to take because ultimately 'you get what you measure'. The various metrics that can be adopted have been discussed and evaluated, highlighting the variable nature of the subject. With this book I hope to have provided you with the information and necessary techniques to make an assessment of your Patent Creation Factory and decide upon the metrics that need to be put in place. Metrics are important as they ultimately act as a means for you to measure the success of your business. Collectively they provide a checklist through which you can ensure the maintenance or continuity of a successful practice, or a means to highlight the reasons behind a specific failure that then requires you to alter a practice in order to improve performance.

Quality is about meeting and exceeding expectations. The quality of your patents will ultimately depend upon the quality of the processes you have in place, which in turn is linked to the quality of the management structure of your factory. Quality must also be seen as an integral part of patent creation leadership and management. If it is embedded in your strategies, daily decisions and actions it will subsequently become the responsibility of everyone in your factory. Quality activities are various and happen at all levels of a Patent Creation Factory, and you need to ensure that common methods and tools, measures and feedback processes are in place to continuously monitor and improve performance. The term quality implies a degree of excellence! Quality relates to patent creation in two ways: first, the quality of your end product or in other words the patent; and second, in relation to the quality of the processes in place and the organisation itself. Patent quality is an important issue and must be ensured across the whole spectrum of patent creation.

Patents and the processes involved in patent creation can be expensive and your costs must be weighed and managed. Cost management involves the planning, coordination, control and reporting of all cost related aspects. It is the process of identifying all costs associated with the investment, making informed choices about the options that will deliver the best value for money and managing those costs throughout the life of patent creation. Decisions about cost must be based on an understanding of the whole supply chain involved and therefore must be weighed against the immense value that patents generate for business. The costs that can be incurred vary considerably from country to country depending on factors such as the nature of the invention, its complexity, attorney fees, plus the length of the application and any objections that might be raised during the examination by the patent office. Therefore it is extremely important to keep in mind and properly manage the costs related to patent creation. Although the cost of obtaining and maintaining a patent may be significant at first, it should be noted that patent costs are only a small fraction of the total cost incurred in turning an invention into a commercially useful product and of marketing and selling it in the relevant market.

A process is an agreement to do certain things in a certain way. The larger the Patent Creation Factory becomes, the more the need for an agreement on ways of working. Processes are the memory of your factory and without them a lot of effort can be wasted by having to start each task from scratch every time and possibly repeating the same mistakes. Processes facilitate good communication between the information originator and receiver, because they help to set and manage expectations and consistency of information. Processes must not be static, because they are in place to serve the Patent Creation Factory and not vice versa. Ways and means to take identified improvements systematically into use should exist within your factory and well-established processes can be used as a tool to do this. Processes define what and how things are done and by whom, to ensure repeatability. They also enable you to set performance criteria and measurement, which can be utilised when identifying the source or root cause of problems or excessive variation in the quality and the output of your Patent Creation Factory.

Tool selection is best tackled once the patent creation processes are defined. You will first need to define and agree your key processes and then select the tools necessary to support these processes. Just as with a traditional factory, proper investment enhances your factory's status as a centre of excellence for the production of patents and helps achieve efficiencies within the production process. And just like a traditional factory that needs various systems, tools and equipment in order to excel, the same applies to your Patent Creation Factory. Bearing in mind the high cost of many of the IP and patent systems and tools needed for the smooth running of your Patent Creation Factory, you need to plan these systems and tools, just as you would with any investment decision. Careful planning is the key to successful long-term investment.

Benchmarking can help to identify if and when changes are needed and the exact nature of those necessary changes, as well as provide an organisation with the courage and conviction to make the changes. It is a process of comparing and contrasting some aspects or elements of an organisation against those of another. It is typically systematic in nature and usually reserved for critical processes given the time and energy needed to conduct a proper and professional benchmarking exercise. The ultimate goal of any such exercise is to gain information that will help the organisation take action to improve its performance, and benchmarking is recognised as one of the most effective means to identify improvements that can make a significant difference to the success of your factory.

Inevitably, there are an abundance of patent change initiatives taking place worldwide and to mention them all would be impossible and is frankly unnecessary. Instead, I have opted to hand pick a variety of examples to discuss in the book, some of which will undoubtedly have a greater effect than others, with the objective of giving you a rough idea on how the patenting world is evolving. Some of the changes described are actually happening while others are still at the discussion and debate stage.

Throughout this book I have written about various subjects relating to the efficient and effective operation of a Patent Creation Factory and highlighting the associated issues to be considered, before discussing the options available. I have on a number of occasions stressed that there are no right or wrong options because circumstances will vary. However, by taking the steps indicated, you should be well on your way to having a world-class Patent Creation Factory.

# Creativity and innovation

Innovation starts with thinking differently. It is a process of questioning, experimenting, learning and adapting. It requires an appetite for risk, a willingness to question, an open mind to look at things without a predetermined conception and perhaps most importantly, patience and perseverance. Innovation is the raw material of your Patent Creation Factory and the quality of your ideas therefore has a direct effect on the outcome and success of what you hope to achieve. It is therefore important that your ideas are of the highest quality and you ensure a steady supply of them. Innovation can take many forms. It can be disruptive, transformative, radical, breakthrough or incremental in nature. The innovation process involves ambiguity, controversy and nonlinearity, and innovation may impact the product, the service, the process or the business model.

> *"Creativity is inventing, experimenting, growing, taking risks, breaking rules, making mistakes, and having fun."*　Mary Lou Cook

Creativity and innovation are key elements to survival and profitability in any business environment. Markets are demanding new products, with better designs and more features at lower prices. Consequently, the effective management of innovation is a vital component of any successful business. Innovation can be the process of creating a new market, which is in the presumed interests of the customer, or it can be making changes to the current provision of a product, in order to better satisfy expressed customer needs. It may be simply improving a product currently on the market and enhancing its overall value to the customer, based on expressed feedback. It is therefore imperative that your inventor community is understood and appreciated, because they supply the innovation, creativity and ideas, which act as the basic raw materials in the Patent Creation Factory.

# Wrap-up

The focus in this book has been on patents, but patents are only one type of IPR and patent creation is only one part of a typical IP organisation. Other elements of IP such as trademarks, designs, domain names and copyright remain very important. What must be kept in mind therefore is that patents are just one of the many rights that exist to protect intangible assets and thus, more than ever, IP is essential in today's market economy. It is also important to take a holistic view of IPR and to realise that the premeditated use of multiple IP regimes can help achieve sustainable differentiation.

> *"It is good to have an end to journey towards, but it is the journey that matters in the end."*
> Ursula K. LeGuin

This book is based on my own experiences of managing and leading a Patent Creation Factory and taking it through some dramatic organisational changes. Time and energy was spent examining our organisational structure and mode of operation, reviewing various options and benchmarking our organisation against others. I also examined the key interfaces of concern to our 'factory'. However, that said, I realise that my knowledge and experience in the field of IP is still very limited. There is still much learning to be done about how best to manage and lead a Patent Creation Factory and I will continue to learn and develop and no doubt make some mistakes along the way. I hope that the writing of this book will mark a key milestone in my own, personal learning journey. I know, most definitely, that I have grown and developed on my journey!

> *"I can no other answer make, but thanks and thanks."*   William Shakespeare

To say that this book is 'by Donal O'Connell' is not exactly the truth. I could not have completed this book without the tremendous advice, contribution, help and support from a great number of people and for that I am extremely grateful.

I wish you well in your quest to establish your world-class Patent Creation Factory and trust that this book helps you greatly in that endeavour.

> *"Twenty years from now you will be more disappointed by the things you didn't do than by the ones you did do. So throw off the bowlines. Sail away from the safe harbor. Catch the trade winds in your sail. Explore. Dream. Discover."* Mark Twain

# References

Source of information of patent facts, figures and trends:

The World Intellectual Property Office (WIPO) Patent Report, 2007 Edition (available at http://www.wipo.int/ipstats/en/statistics/patents/patent_report_2007.html)

Sources of information on the history of patents:

- http://www.historical-markers.org/usptohistory.cgi

- http://www.translationdirectory.com/article835.htm

- http://www.patentlens.net/daisy/patentlens/2648.html

Sources of information on patenting processes and procedures:

- WIPO web site (http://www.wipo.int)

- US Patent and Trademark Office web site

- European Patent Office (EPO) web site

- UK Patent Office web site

- China Patent Office web site

- Japanese Patent Office web site

Sources of information on patent attorney associations:

- CIPA (Chartered Institute of Patent Attorneys) in the UK

- AIPLA (American Intellectual Property Law Association) in the USA

- ACPAA (All-China Patent Agents Association) in China

Sources of information on various patent initiatives:

- European Patent Office Future Scenarios Report

- IBM

- World Business council for Sustainable Development and their Eco Patent Common initiative

Source of information on metrics:

- ISM3

Source of information on patent costs:

- UK Patent Office web site: http://www.ipo.gov.uk/patent

Sources of information on patent quality:

- USPTO

- IBM

- Columbia Law School

- Intellectual Property Owners / August 2005 survey of members

  - http://www.ipo.org/PatentQualityReport

- Research conducted by Assistant Professor of Strategic and International Management at London Business School, Markus Reitzig, and his co-author Paul Burke (University of Technology, Sydney)

Sources of information on innovation:

- Boston Consultancy Group report on innovation – 'Innovation 2006'

Sources of information on motivation:

- Maslow's Hierarchy of Needs

# Index

*Index compiled by Terry Halliday*